Seek The Lover Within

Lessons from 50
Spiritual Leaders

Volume 2

by
Tuula Fai

50 Interviews: Seek the Lover Within: Lessons from 50 Spiritual Leaders (Volume 2)
Copyright © 2010 by Tuula Fai
http://spiritual.50interviews.com

ISBN: 978-1-935689-06-5

Published by
50 Interviews Inc.
Colorado, USA
www.50interviews.com

All rights reserved. No part of this book may be reproduced in any form or by any electronic or mechanical means, including information storage and retrieval systems, without written permission from the author, except in the case of a reviewer, who may quote brief passages embodied in critical articles or in a review.

Trademarked names appear throughout this book. Rather than use a trademark symbol with every occurrence of a trademarked name, names are used in an editorial fashion, with no intention of infringement of the respective owner's trademark.

The information in this book is distributed on an "as is" basis, without warranty. Although every precaution has been taken in the preparation of this work, neither the author nor the publisher shall have any liability to any person or entity with respect to any loss or damage caused or alleged to be caused directly or indirectly by the information contained in this book.

Based on original *50 Interviews* concept by Brian Schwartz.

First edition. Printed in the United States of America.

Dedications

To my grandmother, Sophia Klinker, who gave me unconditional love and passion for life.

To my mother, Elaine Hoiska, who taught me how to write and pursue my dreams.

FOREWORD

Day in and day out we are making choices, many thousands of them over a lifetime: who we call friend, how we make a living, where we live, whether or not we marry, how we spend our money, what kind of a car we drive (or *don't* drive), what we eat, where we go on vacation, what we name our children, how many pets we live with...*whew*...and what kind of a relationship we choose to have (or not have) with God.

Some of our choices may appear to be more important than others. Surely, connecting with *God* trumps adopting a puppy, doesn't it? The nature of our spiritual practice must be more significant than whether we have sweet tea or café mocha during break, isn't it?

In truth, *all* of our choices, even the one to buy the Barcelona red Prius with the navigation package upgrade, or the one to name the new puppy Buddha, or the one to spend our vacation rebuilding homes in Haiti are reflections of who we are, who we've chosen to be. Our choices reveal more about us than any resume, Rorschach inkblot, astrological chart, IQ test, or Facebook quiz. They're full-length mirrors reflecting our thoughts and beliefs back to us. Our choices, whether we deem them good, bad, or otherwise, are ours, and only ours—and they blend together to create a vibrant, multidimensional portrait of us as individual and unique expressions of spirit.

The choices we make affirm and reaffirm what we believe about ourselves, about the world around us, and about the Source of all creation which many of us call God. Our choices may be screaming, "My life is wonderful, amazing, fulfilling, magnificent, and joy filled." They could be telling everyone that we're "getting by" with more good days than bad, but it's an uphill climb. Or they could be reflecting the lyrics in John Mellencamp's classic song, "Jack and Diane" where he laments about life going on long after the thrill of living is gone.

Are we living life fully, struggling from day to day, or simply putting in our time, waiting for the pain of living to finally come to an end? Are our choices telling everyone (including ourselves) that we see life as full and overflowing? As half full? Or as half empty . . . with a slow leak?

What are we reflecting? A spiritually connected life? A life lived from a place of love? A life ruled by fear? Just as we have a choice to read (or not read) this book, we always have a choice to change what we're reflecting.

Choosing to grow spiritually is a courageous decision, one that demands we confront fear in all its forms (hate, anger, prejudice, judgment, guilt, depression, jealousy, self-hatred, and so on) and overcome it through divine love. A spiritual leader is someone who has made that choice, someone who commits to a path that reflects all that is good and empowering, a path that affirms love in all its magnificent expressions.

We are all seekers who aspire to become finders. Sometimes we're not entirely sure what we're seeking, and we don't always recognize it when we find it.

I used to joke that I didn't make a move without first receiving a "sign from God." (God, in turn, joked that I was oblivious to all the signs I was receiving every second of every day.) Then one day, I finally got the punch line. There in front of me, posted in the window of my favorite bookstore, was a *real* sign. It read, "Help Wanted." *You got that right, God*, I thought to myself. As I moved in closer to see what appeared to be another line just beneath the "Help Wanted," I chuckled just a little. "Inquire Within," it said. Help wanted? Inquire within.

What we're all seeking is direction and purpose. To become finders, we need to refocus our search from outside of ourselves to within, to that sacred inner place of divine wisdom.

The spiritual leaders profiled in this book have all "inquired within" in one way or another, and found what they sought... at least in part. Even as "finders" we are led to seek and seek again. We are finders and seekers, finders and seekers, repeating the cycle over and over. But, with each new search, we have a greater understanding of exactly what we're looking for.

Tuula Fai began her journey as a seeker. During her fifty interviews, she has become a finder and a seeker and a finder once again...fifty times (and still counting). What a wonderful experience it is to sit beside Tuula as she engages in question and answer sessions with some of the most fascinating people on the planet; interviews that are often profound, sometimes humorous, occasionally paradigm-shattering, and always inspiring. Each life journey, each "aha" moment shared, is as unique as the spiritual leaders themselves.

Whether Tuula realizes it or not, the very process of putting together these two volumes has made her a spiritual leader. She has chosen to commit to a path that reflects the best she can be, a path of empowerment that has turned her from a seeker to a finder of the lover within.

-Linda M. Potter
Author of If God Would Only Give Me a Sign!

CONTENTS

Laleh Bakhtiar, Author of *The Sublime Quran* 1

Valentina Borodina, Medical Intuitive, Scientist, and Healer ... 9

Tamara Bowman Mooers, President, Emerald Echo, the Resort. Author, *Living on the Edge of Goodbye* and *Emerald Echo-The Story* 21

Chad Cameron, Leap! Ventures LLC 35

Pamela Chapman, iAscend Programs, LLC 41

Jason Chen, Chinese Intuitive and Fortune-Teller 47

Father Tom Coyte, Priest, Holy Cross Catholic Church 55

Ann Cunningham, Sculptor, Multi-Sensory Artist, and Author 63

Hale Dwoskin, The Sedona Method 71

Alicia Fall, Founder of Her Many Voices 81

Jamy Faust, Cofounder, Healing Arts of Belmont 87

Hugh Halter, Community Missionary and Author of *The Tangible Kingdom* 95

Hank Innerfeld, Spiritual Healer, Speaker, Teacher, and Author 101

Reverend Cynthia James, Mile Hi Church 117

Lisa Jones, Best Selling Author and Journalist 125

Skip Lackey, Senior Journey Trainer and Practitioner, North America 139

Jill Lublin, Speaker, Strategist, Author, and Radio & TV Host 153

Rabbi Anat Moskowitz, Religion Professor, Colorado College and Rabbi, Congregation B'nai Torah 159

Eric Moya, Esalen and The Upledger Institute 167

Mike Parker, Poet, Painter, Musician, and Mountaineer 173

The Rev. Diana Peters, Intercession Episcopal Church.......... 185

Denye Robbins, Cofounder, Journeys for Conscious Living .. 193

Dr. Lewis Ryder, Honorary Senior Lecturer in Physics,
University of Kent 203

Elias Salem, A New Monday Life Coaching 211

Linda Sloan, Author and
Cofounder of The Transformation Group 217

Janet Solyntjes, The Center for Courageous Living............... 223

Terri Starck, LifePoint Strategies 231

Eddie Yau, Secondary English Teacher,
Pentecostal Lam Hon Kwong School..................................... 235

"I am a part of all that I have met."

-Alfred Lord Tennyson, *Ulysses*

INTRODUCTION

In Book One of *Seek the Lover Within*, I told the story of how a crippling injury put me on my spiritual path. I also shared that my main spiritual practice is choosing love over fear. I do this by noticing when I am fearful and then using the Hawaiian practice of ho'oponopono and Gary Zukav's and Linda Francis' Spiritual Partnership Guidelines to clear it. I especially draw upon these tools when dealing with perceived enemies. They help me see that the only real enemy is my own distorted perception.

In this volume, I am going to talk about my challenges with choosing love. I want to share them to show that becoming the spiritual leader of your life isn't easy. It takes practice. Writing this book series was part of my practice. It helped me transition from thinking about choosing love to actually doing it. Now I see that every moment, we have the opportunity to grow in love or contract in fear. Through my example, I want you to persevere in choosing love. You may have to try several times before you can do so consistently. That's okay. The universe doesn't care how many tries it takes. It only cares that you eventually do it.

In fact, I myself ended up writing two books instead of one because I needed to gain more experience. The more leaders I interviewed, the more questions I had. The more answers I received, the more I understood what it means to choose love. I had to keep going until I felt the leaders' teachings become a way of life. Only then could I effectively convey these ideas.
With these teachings now part of me, both books are infused with a message of love. You can pick up either one and directly learn from my experience and that of the spiritual leaders. Or you can pick up both and walk the journey with me. The choice is yours.

Childhood

Before diving into my challenges with choosing love, I want to share a bit about my childhood. These early experiences will help explain some of my fears and how they impact my relationships.

When I was fourteen, my parents separated. They moved to different states, leaving my brother in private school and me in our old house. The first year, I lived with a family who rented our home. When they moved out, I began raising myself. Although I felt abandoned, I had the support of my first love, Andy, whose caring helped me cope.

I was devastated when Andy moved to India senior year. I thought, *Love is unreliable. Instead, I'll focus on achievement. At least no one can take that away from me.* Thus began my descent into workaholism. I worked hard at everything, from academics and athletics to networking and socializing. However, no amount of work could heal my lack of self-worth and fear of abandonment. In fact, this way of avoiding the pain only made it worse.

When I married my husband, I saw how compulsive I had been. He would angrily say, "You never think of me. You think only about your work." He was right, but his anger scared me and I retreated ever further. Then our son was born and my heart slowly began to open.

Challenges
It was at this time that my in-laws came to live with us for six-month periods. My husband is from Hong Kong, where it is common for extended families to live together. As a result, he was happy with the arrangement but I was not. So my first challenge with choosing love was embracing my new family.

Living with them was tough on many levels. I was used to having privacy and doing things my way. Now I had to share space and make compromises. Beneath this surface challenge was the deeper issue of my fear. Ironically, I feared both intimacy and abandonment. *I won't let myself care about you because you'll just leave me.* This false belief stemmed from my lack of self-worth. Since I didn't love myself, how could I expect anyone else to?

Interactions with my in-laws and husband triggered this fear. For example, my in-laws often gave me advice and assistance around the house. My fear made me think they were questioning my competence and I grew frustrated and impatient. Also, my father-in-law often got angry with my mother-in-law. When he did, he would shout and then ignore her until his temper cooled. One night, he shouted so much that she yelled back at him right in front of my husband, son, and me.

This incident happened a few hours before I attended Lynne McTaggart's lecture on consciousness experiments at The International Society for the Study of Subtle Energies and Energy Medicine. As I drove to her talk, I realized I was using the lecture as an excuse to withdraw in fear. I found myself resenting my father-in-law for his anger and my mother-in-law for her submissiveness.

I was still thinking about this when the opening act came on stage. It was a Tibetan singing bowl healer named Shree Krishna Shahi. By coincidence, I had just given a CranioSacral Therapy session to a woman from Hawaii and her daughter. When I told them I was writing this book, they suggested I go to the Old Tibet store and interview a man who was visiting from Nepal. It turned out this singing bowl healer was that man. I thought it was a sign, so I called Old Tibet and scheduled the interview.

In meeting Shree, I was immediately struck by his open heart and gentle spirit. During his interview, it became clear that he truly wished to heal as many people as possible. Being in his presence helped me relax and open on all levels. Intuitive Penney Peirce (interviewed in Book One) says we often feel like this when we meet people who vibrate at a similar frequency. That certainly was the case for me because I left the interview feeling happy and peaceful.

When I returned home, I discovered that tensions had reached the breaking point. My father-in-law was threatening to leave my mother-in-law and I shut down in fear. I was tired of dealing with their drama and just wanted out. I spoke to my husband, but he just shrugged his shoulders and said, "Children from Asia don't question their parents. Besides, they will be gone in a few months."

A few months. I'll never make it!

This wasn't the first time I had felt this way. Earlier that year, I had stormed out of a restaurant while visiting my husband's family in China. Anyone familiar with Chinese culture knows that "losing face" in this way is one of the worst crimes a person can commit—and I had done it with gusto. I even whispered under my breath "freaking Chinese people." So much for loving my enemy!

I knew I needed help with the situation, so I called psychotherapist and healer Jamy Faust (interviewed in this book). I told her about my reactions to my in-laws and husband, and we discussed possible solutions. The obvious one was opening my heart and sharing my feelings with them. The other was leaving the situation. Since I had run most of my life, I decided that the loving choice would be to open my heart and get us help.

I began by asking Shree to give my in-laws Tibetan singing bowl therapy. My father-in-law was so much calmer after his session that I went back a week later to learn the therapy myself. When I arrived, Shree demonstrated how to play the bowls for total body balancing. Then he lay down and asked me to practice giving him sound therapy. I felt a little unsure but gave it a go. After a few minutes, Shree got up and said, "Tuula, you gave me exactly what I needed. I had to get up because I was falling into too deep a meditation and I wouldn't be able to teach. You really have a touch for this."

It was very healing to be acknowledged in this way—so much so that I began to cry. I then shared with Shree what I had been going through at home and we talked about it for a while. We then continued the lesson by striking the bowls and chanting. I had never chanted before so I did the best I could. Again, Shree said, "You have no idea when I tell you how many thousands of students I have trained. Your chanting is very good. You can make a CD."

Shree's encouragement gave me the confidence to start using the bowls right away in my CranioSacral Therapy practice. Incorporating them seemed so natural that I wondered why more practitioners weren't doing so. Many months later, I discovered that CranioSacral Therapy originated in Tibet where it is often practiced with singing bowls. I was excited to learn this because I could see how much progress my clients were making.

Up to this point, my experience with Shree had been entirely positive. Then came challenge number two: I developed romantic feelings for him. I thought about him all the time and even imagined what it would be like to touch him. I knew these thoughts were inappropriate so I tried to shut them down. The more I tried, the stronger they became. I soon realized that I was falling into a familiar pattern of savior-seeking. By this I mean that I was looking for a white knight to rescue me from my pain. Somehow finding this knight would magically heal my lack of self-worth and fear of intimacy and abandonment.

When I arrived at my last singing bowl session, Shree said, "I knew you were coming. I hadn't read the schedule, but my heart told me so. Do you understand?"

I didn't but I was so confused by my feelings that I just said, "Yes," and turned my attention to playing the bowls. During the lesson, I said, "Shree, when I finish this book series, do you think you could play a concert at one of my talks?"

Shree replied, "Yes. Together we can help so many people."

When he said this, I felt a rift between my personality and my soul. My soul agreed with him and wanted to heal as many people as possible. However, the "frightened parts of my personality" (term used by Gary Zukav and Linda Francis) coveted him. I knew I couldn't create anything good from fear, so I asked God to release me from my unhealthy desire. This worked temporarily. We finished the lesson and hugged good-bye.

The last time I saw Shree was at a concert where he and his colleague Santa played. During the show, I vacillated between falling into deep meditation and suffering with desire. Shree was returning to Nepal and I wouldn't see him for another year . . . or maybe never again. The pain was so intense that I went outside to get some air. As I sat under a tree, a fox approached me. Native American musician Alicia Fall (interviewed in this book) told me that foxes teach us how to walk in both worlds and between them. I thanked the fox for supporting me as I released an energetic cord that had bound me to Shree and my savior-seeking pattern.

The next week I came across three books that helped me understand what was going on. They were *Becoming Enlightened* by the Dalai Lama, *This Moment is the Perfect Teacher* by Pema Chödrön, and *Broken: A Love Story* by Lisa Jones (interviewed in this book). Whenever I felt lust for Shree, I would read Becoming Enlightened and its teachings would immediately shift my perspective. I would remember that life is an impermanent illusion, but one in which every choice I make counts. As Gandhi said, "Whatever you do will seem insignificant, but it is important that you do it."

So each time I felt the desire to savior-seek, I would recommit to choosing thoughts and actions that would bring others and myself happiness, not suffering. I appreciated these teachings because they were like an operating manual for living the Ten Commandments.

I then listened to *This Moment is the Perfect Teacher* by Pema Chödrön, in which she says we can use the three poisons of lust, hatred, and ignorance as medicine to bring us closer to enlightenment. We do so by going into the pain and allowing it to open and transform us. Medicine man Stanford Addison echoed her sentiments in the book *Broken: A Love Story*, in which he says, "What's bad is good. It helps you find your center."

Their teachings made a lot of sense to me. I had chosen a higher level of pain so I could wake up instead of sleepwalking through life. Heck, I'd done it once before when a crippling injury encouraged me to grow and heal two decades earlier (see Book One's introduction for details).

This understanding was so new, however, that I felt I needed further support. As a result, I signed up for Gary Zukav's and Linda Francis' Living Courageously workshop. In the seminar, I learned about authentic power. Authentic power is the alignment of my personality with my soul. It enables me to choose loving thoughts and actions so I can live my soul's intentions of harmony, cooperation, sharing, and reverence for life. I practiced creating authentic power by using the Spiritual Partnership Guidelines. These guidelines of commitment, courage, compassion, and conscious communications and actions helped me choose love instead of fear.

For example, committing to my spiritual growth means paying attention to how I react in situations. If I feel uncomfortable physical sensations around my seven chakras (energy centers), I know a "frightened part of my personality" is active. If I were to act upon it, I would create destructive consequences. Instead, I challenge this fear by fully feeling it and then using courage and compassion to act from the most loving part of myself. I do this by consulting my intuition, setting my intention, and speaking personally and specifically without attachment to the outcome.

This practice was so powerful when I first tried it that I joined Zukav's and Francis' three-year Authentic Power Program. In the program, I have learned that the more I challenge a "frightened part of my personality," the more it loses control over me. And the more I cultivate a "loving part of my personality," the more it becomes part of my awareness and experience. Using the Spiritual Partnership Guidelines has enabled me to choose love more often, so I live with less fear.

This practice came at just the right time for challenge number three: learning to love my husband. To help us with our intimacy, he and I began seeing Ron Aarons, a psychotherapist with a spiritual approach to couples counseling. At our first session Ron said to me, "So let me get this straight. You're writing a book series about loving everyone, even your adversaries, yet you view your own husband as the enemy?"

"Yes," I replied. "Ironic isn't it?"

After having a good laugh Ron asked, "What is the most loving thing you could do right now for Jasper?"

My first thought was to establish some sort of physical contact. So I got up and went to sit with him in his chair. I felt very uncomfortable at first. My throat and chest tightened as my heart struggled to open. I also felt like I wanted to run or, at the very least, distract myself by talking. Instead, I decided to challenge these "frightened parts" by sitting with my feelings and asking Jasper if I could hold his hand. He said, "Yes," and we continued to sit, just softening into each other. The longer I sat, the more peaceful I became. Eventually, my heart started to open.

Ron asked if it would be helpful to say the ho'oponopono phrase, "I love you. I am sorry. Please forgive me. Thank you."

I said, "Absolutely." So for many minutes, the three of us said the phrase to cleanse our fears.

In the sessions that followed, Jasper and I took turns exploring our "frightened parts" and seeing their effect on our relationship. We felt their physical sensations and then challenged these "parts" by sharing our feelings and committing to more loving interactions. This exploration helped us see each other as spiritual partners. According to Zukav and Francis, a spiritual partnership is a partnership between equals for the purpose of spiritual growth. Now Jasper and I help each other create authentic power (choose love) by using the Spiritual Partnership Guidelines to deepen our relationship.

Choosing Love
In the introduction to Book One, I said I had chosen the spiritual leaders in this series because they listen to the God within and act from this place. This enables them to consciously choose love rather than fear. In so doing, they create beneficial experiences for themselves and everyone around them. To me, this is what it means to be the spiritual leader of your life.

In this introduction, I am sharing my personal challenges to help you see that becoming a spiritual leader doesn't happen overnight. It happens with each decision you make. Don't take my word for it. You can see the transformative power of love in the lives of the spiritual leaders in this book.

For example, author Laleh Bakhtiar used the pain of divorce to deepen her Muslim faith (Sufism) and write the first English translation of the Quran by an American woman. Russian intuitive Valentina Borodina allowed her son's death to teach her how to love more deeply. Rabbi Anat Moskowitz's experience with breast cancer enabled her to be more authentic and present. Father Tom Coyte's introverted nature helped him cultivate love for others and himself. Hugh Halter's sister's mental illness gave him compassion for the people he ministers to in the streets. And Eddie Yau's shyness and feelings of inferiority encouraged him to connect with other spiritual men.

As Zukav says, the more we choose love, the more authentically powerful we become. When we do not choose love, we unconsciously act from the "frightened parts of our personalities," thereby creating the same painful consequences over and over again.

Free yourself from fear by recognizing and challenging your "frightened parts." One of the best times to do this is when you are upset. Instead of distancing yourself from the pain, stop and explore what you are feeling. Focus on the physical sensations in your body near your seven chakras. If any are uncomfortable, you know that a "frightened part of your personality" is active. You also know that you now have an opportunity to choose love.

Do so by connecting to the lover within and asking what you should do. Then open your heart and mind to really listen. When the intuition comes, set the intention to act from the most loving part of yourself. This involves accepting responsibility for your experience and speaking about it without attachment. It often helps me to combine this practice with saying the ho'oponopono phrase, "I love you. I am sorry. Please forgive me. Thank you."

Again, it may take several tries before you can consistently choose love. As astronaut Charlie Duke (interviewed in Book One) says, ". . . don't get discouraged . . . persevere because the Lord is there." The divinity within is always with you. It doesn't care how many times you choose fear. All that matters is that, at some point, you choose love. When you do, it will be there to help. Skip Lackey of Brandon Bay's The Journey (interviewed in this book) says, "When you take a step towards grace, it takes 1,000 steps towards you."

Your journey begins right now by committing to your spiritual growth, by having the courage and compassion to consciously choose loving thoughts and actions. Start by reading the stories of these spiritual leaders' lives. They will inspire you to fall madly in love with your own life. They will help you see that you are a precious child of God in whom boundless potential dwells. You can release this potential by choosing love. The more you love yourself and others, the greater service you are to the world. When you live from love, following your calling becomes effortless. You know who you are and what you have come to do. Now do it with love.

To Life!
Tuula Fai, Denver, Colorado
Valentine's Day 2011

"In becoming Muslim, I didn't lose Jesus. I gained Muhammad."
Laleh Bakhtiar, Author of *The Sublime Quran*

Laleh Bakhtiar is the coauthor of *A Sense of Unity: The Sufi Tradition in Persian Architecture* and author of *Sufi Expressions of the Mystic Quest, God's Will Be Done: Traditional Psychoethics and Personality Paradigm* (three volumes), and fifteen other books on Islam. She has translated over thirty books on the Islamic movement into English and is the first American woman to translate the Quran. She travels around the world giving lectures on Muslim women's rights. She is a leading authority on the Sufi origins of the enneagram and the psychology of spiritual chivalry—*futuwwa* and *javanmardi*. She directs her work towards Muslim women and youth.

She currently is the director of the Institute of Traditional Psychology and an in-house scholar at KAZI Publications. She has taught Islam at the University of Chicago, has an online learning program at www.sufienneagram.com, and is a nationally certified counselor and Licensed Professional Psychotherapist in the State of Illinois. She earned a doctorate in educational psychology, two master's degrees in counseling psychology and philosophy, and a bachelor's degree in history.

Q. What experiences put you on your spiritual path?
A. My mother was an American Christian and my father was an Iranian Muslim. They eventually divorced and my mother raised me here in the United States. I attended Catholic school and converted to the faith when I was eight. Even though my mother wasn't Catholic, she supported my decision. Growing up, I spent a lot of time alone because my mother was busy caring for my six older siblings. During that period, I became very interested in studying religion.

Later on, I married an Iranian man and we went to live in Tehran. There I reunited with my father, who had returned to his home country, and met a spiritual mentor named Seyyed Hossein Nasr. Nasr felt that people would expect me to be Muslim since I lived in Iran and both my father and husband were Iranian. I told him, "But I don't know anything about Islam," to which he replied, "Well, learn." So I began studying Islam with him through the path of Sufism. For me, there is not much distinction between Catholicism and Islam. They both talk about love of God. I tell people, "In becoming Muslim, I didn't lose Jesus. I gained Muhammad." Having learned about both was essential to my development.

Q. How did these experiences change you?
A. They changed me in the sense of wanting to be the best moral person I could be. Morality has always been important to me. I raised my children to value honesty, responsibility, and hard work. I taught them to be grateful to God for their blessings and to accept when things don't go their way. This requires submission and an understanding that God knows what's best for them.

Q. What has been the most challenging part of your path?
A. When my husband of sixteen years asked for a divorce. He traveled a lot for work and had met someone on one of his trips. I had no idea the split was coming. That's what made it so devastating. I also didn't have a way to earn a living because I hadn't worked since marrying and having children. Two years after our divorce, the Iranian Revolution happened. The revolution, by comparison, was easy for me. I thought, *I've been through worse than this!* My unexpected divorce was definitely the most difficult experience of my life.

Q. Who are your mentors? What have you learned from them?
A. My first mentor was my former husband, who was an architect. Prior to meeting him, I had studied history and didn't

know much about the creative world. He introduced me to this world through his poetic vision of architecture. We later coauthored a book called *The Sense of Unity: The Sufi Tradition in Persian Architecture.* It's still in print because no one has been able to refine or refute its concepts. My main spiritual mentor was Seyyed Hossein Nasr, who taught me about Sufism. I met him when he lived in Iran before the 1979 revolution. He showed me that Sufism is the path of love to God. Nasr is currently a professor at George Washington University.

Q. What is the greatest challenge facing society?
A. Divisiveness. Instead of dividing ourselves up into different faiths—Christians, Jews, Muslims, Hindus, Buddhists—we should focus on our common ideas and ways of life. Divine revelations have come to all peoples, regardless of religion. So each of us has an obligation to distinguish between right and wrong and speak out against injustice, especially when governments preserve the status quo to maintain their own power. Throughout history, the prophets have given us this message but we have not been able to follow it for any length of time. After a few years, the priestly function of government always seems to undermine justice and unity. Right now, the media has an opportunity to promote justice by informing people about what's going on in places like Iran. President Obama seems to be doing this too. This is hopeful because, in the past, we have had a tendency to cover things up.

Q. What is your earliest memory? Why do you remember it?
A. When I was three years old, we lived in Los Angeles during World War II. After the bombing of Pearl Harbor, the city had blackouts every night in case the Japanese attacked the mainland. My mother was a nurse and worked nights. So my two older sisters took care of me. Before they put me to sleep at night, I would always check in my closet and under my bed to make sure no Japanese were hiding there. Need-

less to say, I never found any!

Q. What advice would you give someone just starting his or her spiritual path?
A. I would ask if they have a particular faith. If they do, I would ask why they follow it. Is it out of genuine belief or an obligation to their parents? If they are just imitating their parents, then I would advise them to go out and study other religions. This process will help bring consciousness to what they believe. It's not acceptable to mimic others. We each need to find our own truth, whether it's in our family's tradition or a different one.

Q. What are your practices for connecting to your higher purpose?
A. Being Muslim, I pray five times a day. I also belong to a Sufi order in which we do the Remembrance of God Liturgy. I find these practices spiritually uplifting. I also enjoy writing because I always end up discussing Islam or some other religion or way of life. Translating the Quran was a great blessing because it really enhanced my faith. In Islam, the greatest sin is to forget God. So I try to remember God in everything I do—eating, sleeping, and so forth. Of course, I don't always remember. But that's my goal, to start everything in the name of God.

Q. How do you use these practices when you get out of balance?
A. I use the Sufi integration of the enneagram to help me heal morally and ethically. Each night I look at the nine-point diagram[1] to assess where I am within myself. For example, if I was angry or jealous that day, then I must apologize to the offended party. After apologizing a few times, I realized that doing that was harder than restraining myself in the first place. So I started to develop awareness around when I got angry, so I could better control it. In this way, I use the ennea-

---

[1]George Ivanovich Gurdjieff brought this diagram to the West in the 1920s.

gram to reason with myself and morally heal along the nine outer points of the circle.

In the circle's center is the zero point. This point represents Justice—one of Plato's four virtues—and is the entryway into the world of intuition. According to the Sufi poet Rumi, you can reach this point once you have morally healed. However, he says that you cannot take reason with you. This is because intuition is so much larger than reason. It would be like trying to take a lighted candle into the noonday desert sun. Yet we must spend a great deal of our lives using reason to morally heal so we can enter this center point into intuition. Of course, people who have not morally healed have intuitions. The problem is that after a few intuitions, they are pulled back out into one of the nine numbers on the circle's circumference. This is because they have too much or too little of one of the virtues.

I describe the Sufi integration of the enneagram in my three-volume work, *God's Will Be Done*. The Sufis adopted it in the thirteenth century (originated with Aristotle and Plato) because Islam integrates all spiritual texts that existed before the seventh century, as long as they don't go against the oneness of God. That's why the Old and New Testaments and Taoist and Hindu principles are all part of the Islamic tradition.

Today's psychology offers many wonderful techniques such as self-talk, role-playing, and doubling. These are great ways of helping bring people to consciousness. But they lack theory. That's because theory belongs to the traditional world of Judaism, Christianity, Islam, Hinduism, Buddhism, Taoism, and so forth.

Q. How do you balance planning with remaining open to opportunity?
A. This depends on a person's work. Mine happens to be writ-

ing. So I first reason through what I want to do. Then I create some sort of outline or structure. With this scaffolding in place, I can then enter the world of intuition—exploring where things go and how I should say them. Translating the Quran was like this. I received so many intuitive insights while working on it.

Q. If you received $100,000, how would you spend it?
A. If God blessed me with this money, I would work on translating the Quran into different languages because it's important for Muslims to understand that verse 4:34 does not say that husbands can beat their wives. I have had many discussions with Islamic scholars and none of them have been able to refute my argument. It is based on sound criteria I've developed.

Since many in the Muslim world cannot read or write, I would create a CD or DVD of the translation that could be listened to and recited by both women and men. I would give these recordings away for free so that Muslim women could learn about the real meaning of this verse and others. This knowledge would help them gain consciousness of the word of God in the Quran.

Q. If you had thirty seconds with someone in an elevator, what three things would you tell the person to do to be joyful, peaceful, and whole?
A. I would say, "Start searching for the truth. Search for water to quench your thirst." Rumi tells a beautiful story of two men who go into the desert and run out of water. One digs shallow in ten or fifteen places and dies of thirst. The other digs deep in one spot, finds water, and is saved. Your spot may be your family's faith or another tradition. Whatever it is, dig deep. Don't be discouraged if you don't find the answer at first. Just keep digging. You'll find it if you go deep within yourself.

Q. What books or resources have helped you the most? Why?
A. Recommending books and resources depends on where people happen to be in their lives. For example, a highly rational or cognitive person might need to get in touch with nature by taking a walk or planting a garden. However, someone who is already earthy might need the opposite. They might need more reason and interaction with others. Still another person might lack confidence and would benefit from doing self-talk. Whatever the issue, the person must dig deep to discover why they are unhappy and why they might be trying to mask the pain with drugs, alcohol, or whatever else it might be. Sometimes people can find the root cause on their own. Others times, they need help. Psychology offers a lot of resources, as does the traditional world of faith. For example, in Islam there are physicians of the heart called Hakīms. You can talk to them and they will listen and help you. So having a Hakīm or good friend with whom you can share is very important. It's hard to do life alone. We're born alone and we die alone but we don't have to live alone.

Q. What would you like to be written on your tombstone?
A. I think everybody wants a legacy. That's why we have children, grandchildren, and great-grandchildren. We want to touch their hearts in some way or another. Professionally, I would like my legacy to be *The Sublime Quran*. I had remarkable intuitions while doing it that make for an accurate and unique translation, one that is different from other English translations. So I would like to be remembered for that.

Q. How can we in America best foster peace with Iran?
A. If we believe in democracy and peace (not that we always live up to this standard), then we should support the media in reporting what's going on in Iran. Young Iranians, who make up over fifty percent of the population, are trying to establish democracy. We should not interfere with this process because that gives ammunition to the other side. However, our media can help us better understand Iranian culture.

As Dr. Shirin Ebadi, 2003 Nobel Peace Prize winner points out, there are many different kinds of Iranians, each with a unique religion and way of life. So the Iranian people are not monolithically bad or good. We need to understand this and support those Iranians who speak out against injustice, even those from the other side.

For example, President Mahmoud Ahmadinejad is not a popular figure in the West because he says very disturbing things like, "The Holocaust is a myth." However, what he says about the Palestinian plight is basically true. So here is a case in which someone from the other side is saying something true. In this instance, we should support him in gaining justice for the Palestinians.

Q. Anything else?
A. When people read *The Sublime Quran*, they should open it and read a verse at a time. That's because it's more intuitive than historical. I did the translation to help Muslims better understand the word of God. This is important because some Iranian women in the organization Women's Islamic Initiative in Spirituality and Equality (WISE) don't want to work through the Islam faith for political change. They just want Iran to immediately become a secular state. Daisy Khan, WISE's founder, says if we push for a secular state, we won't make inroads because we will leave the people behind. We have to speak to the people in their own language, the language of the Quran and the Islamic faith. Hopefully, over time, they will grow to think as we do.

"Everything is made of love."
Valentina Borodina, Medical Intuitive, Scientist, and Healer

Valentina Borodina is an internationally known healer, medical intuitive, therapist, teacher, scientist, and writer. Valentina was born and has lived much of her life in southwest Siberia. From an early age, her grandmother trained her in the traditional arts of herbology and healing, which later expanded to include homeopathy and bioenergetic healing through gentle body adjustments. The depths of love, the unclaimed gifts of the soul, and a knowing of God arise from her work.

Valentina enhanced the traditional methods she'd already been taught through her medical education and research. In 1981, she received a master's degree in anatomy, physiology, and psychology. From 1982 to 1986, she studied in the Medical Research Institute at the Medical Academy of Russia. In 1985, while working on her PhD in medical biochemistry at the government's Cardiology Scientific and Medical Center in Moscow, she began research into how heart failure, multi-organ toxicity, and other health disorders affect body systems. Herbs became the key, linking allopathic and alternative forms of medicine. Valentina proceeded to study the effects of toxicity and stress on the physical system and how energy healing can restore the body to its natural cycles for greater balance and wellness.

For the past thirty years, Valentina has been teaching and sharing her gifts with people around the globe. Currently, she divides her time between her private practice in America, Canada, and Europe, her international workshops, and her charitable organization in Russia, which serves as a bridge of love between Russia and America.

Q. What experiences put you on your spiritual path?

A. I grew up in Siberia close to my grandmother. She used to read the Bible and talk to me about God. Even though I did not believe in God at the time, I still listened, and her words stayed with me. I was also using my knowledge and intuition, but I didn't think they were anything special. I thought everyone had the same abilities I did. So my grandmother's teachings and my intuitive abilities helped put me on my path. Some years later, my brother died when he was twenty-seven. For half a year, I was not really here. I had gone to the broader world to find him. When I came back, everything in Russia was opening up. It was the time of Gorbachev and glasnost. Parts of metaphysical books were starting to appear in some magazines. I was reading quotes by Richard Bach and other spiritual writers. God came into my life as a true knowingness. Something was pushing me forward and I ended up moving from Siberia to Moscow. From there, everything opened to me.

Q. How did these experiences change you?

A. My brother died when I was in Siberia doing my PhD in biochemistry and making plans to move to Moscow. After disappearing with him for half a year (I was kind of there living my life, walking around, doing things, but I wasn't really there), I returned with a newfound resolve to go to Moscow. I initially thought I would go there to do scientific work, but when I arrived, people kept talking to me about my intuitive abilities and telling me I had something special. The greater openness in Russia led to spiritual leaders forming schools that taught people about healing. I did not know it at the time, but I had already been doing my metaphysical work for years. I also was starting to realize that not everyone had the same vision and feelings of life and people that I did.

Q. What changes were you noticing about your life and the world?

A. My boyfriend in Moscow was always telling me that I had

a unique healing gift. He had asthma. I would work on him and he would feel better. But I still thought my healing hands weren't turned on, and that I needed to find a way to get them working. I even read a book titled, *I Am Listening to My Hands*, written by a well-known Russian healer named Eugenia Davitashvili (Juna). Then one day my boyfriend was on the balcony hanging laundry when he fell off and landed on the sharp side of a metal wash bucket. Parts of his body were swollen black and dark blue and he was in great pain. I had no time to think about whether my hands were working or not. I just started helping him. He completely healed within a day or two. So this boyfriend's fall helped me turn on my hands and become fully conscious of my gift. You know, when you really need to help someone, you don't think about it. You just do it. In fact, the less you think about it, the more successful you are.

Q. What changes were others noticing about you?
A. When my youngest son died five years ago, I could have stayed heartbroken forever. Instead, God and my son helped me use the experience to become more of who I am—more than I had ever been. If I'd stayed in pain, it would have been hard for my son's soul to bear. So I asked him, over and over again, to help me awaken to a deeper consciousness and to learn the true meaning of our existence on this planet. It worked the same way after my brother died, only I wasn't aware of it at the time. Everything we experience comes back to us like a wave. Each time the wave returns we have the opportunity to see and understand it a new way.

Q. What has been the most challenging part of your path?
A. My life has not been easy. I had my first son when I was unmarried and still in high school. Like the deaths of my brother and youngest son, this event could have broken me. Instead, it helped make me stronger. It added to my awareness that support is all around us and is always available. It is never too late to take anything that has happened in the past and use

it as a strength. Nothing has to remain a painful trauma. You can draw power from it to move forward.

Q. What is your earliest memory? Why do you remember it?
A. I had a happy, simple childhood playing with the other kids in the village. I remember my grandmother teaching me about herbs, which ones to eat and which ones to use in healing. Very often, I realized that I already knew the things she was telling me. But at the time I believed that every kid knew them as well. When I was five or six, I remember my mother talking with a neighbor who was trying to get pregnant. I was listening and wanted to tell her that she would conceive if she slept with her husband and drank her urine the next morning. I remember this because I wanted to tell her so badly, even though I didn't even know what sleeping with her husband meant. (I didn't know about sexual intercourse at that age.) Something similar happened when I was eleven and overheard a pregnant woman standing outside the store saying that she'd just seen her doctor about her swollen legs. I wanted to tell her to follow her doctor's advice because the swelling was all over her body and was adversely affecting her baby. But as in the last example, something told me not to say anything. Who would have listened? I was a child.

When I was eighteen, I started to speak the intuitions that were coming to me and learned very quickly that people did not always want to listen, especially when they were not asking for help. But I just couldn't stop because it was harder to stop than to keep going, to keep working on people all the time. So one of my greatest challenges has always been knowing when to use this knowledge and when to remain silent.

Q. Who are your mentors? What have you learned from them?
A. Although it wasn't conscious on my part, I stayed away from schools and books with particular teachings. Even with authors like Richard Bach, I read only a few pages—just enough

to collect little reminders or sparks of insight. This is because I wanted my knowledge to come directly from God and my intuition. When I first came to America, people here said that I knew things they were reading about. Only I hadn't learned them from a book. They also said I knew things that hadn't been written about yet. Of course, now there is so much information that it can be hard to tell what comes from outside and what comes from within. But even when it comes from outside, I still pay attention to how it feels inside me. What I focus on most is teaching people to trust their intuition so they don't just accept something because it comes from an influential source. I call this practice teaching love. It's about knowing that God—and everything around us—directly speaks to us, giving us encouragement, hope, and support.

Q. What is the greatest challenge facing society?
A. Fear—because we don't know how not to be afraid. We teach our children to fear to keep them safe. But they end up being afraid even of love, the thing they desire most. Fear keeps us from being with God, others, and ourselves. We think it's about something external, a crisis or disease, but it's really just fear itself—the fear of how bad things could be. Pain is similar to fear. It just has a different appearance. We must remember that everything is love. Love can cure any crisis, disease, or pain.

When I was young, I didn't really believe in fear. I think many children are like this and some stay this way longer than others. My younger son was like that. He did things no matter what. His bravery was a kind of freedom—a freedom from the heaviness we sometimes carry. We shouldn't teach our children to fear and they shouldn't believe us when they hear it. We need to be free, without limits. Hearing people's stories, like those in this book, will make this freedom come alive for people. It is our greatest treasure.

Q. What advice would you give someone just starting his or her spiritual path?

A. Most people who ask for spiritual advice are trying to make a decision about what to do next. They often place more weight on the decision than it actually has. I would ask them to remember what they would have done as a child. This helps bring out their true nature and inner freedom so they can make the best choice. Right now, there are many resources available to people seeking advice: psychologists, priests, metaphysical practitioners, and so on. The first thing anyone giving advice should learn is how to do no harm, how not to say anything that could damage the person. For example, I have a client who went to see an astrologer because she wanted help in finding love and getting married. The astrologer told her that her chart did not show marriage in this lifetime. She was devastated.

I would never say something like this to a person, even if it were written all over her chart. Instead, I would help her see the good things that are there and develop them so they will become her life. I would also say that if I tell her anything that is painful to hear, then it is probably not from my highest spiritual self—because God would not talk like that. And that she should just be patient because I'll say something in a little while that will support her better. In fact, I encourage everyone to disregard anything they hear that takes away their power and belief in themselves. All of us need to recognize that we may not be the best person to give the truth, and that some words simply shouldn't be said. In order to be of highest service, we need to learn what to listen to and what to say.

Q. What are your practices for connecting to your higher purpose?

A. As I mentioned, my grandmother was always talking to me about God. But at the time, very few children in Russia believed in God. Then in my early thirties, I had the chance to experience God's presence in a way I had never felt before. It was August on my thirty-first birthday. In Russia, people give you flowers on your birthday and I had come home carrying all these bouquets and feeling sad for some reason. When I opened the door, I flopped down on the couch with the flowers and started to cry. Then I felt their petals touching me with warmth, love, and support, almost as if they had human hands. I felt their love and I knew it was from God. Now I know that this love is always there for me in whatever I do—teaching classes, healing clients, or just being with people. Even in the most desperate times, it's there. It may be just a little harder to feel. To me, this love feels like a waterfall flowing behind me that is made of light that connects me with God.

Q. How do you use these practices when you get out of balance?
A. God is always there, even when I am not feeling his presence. Fortunately, my husband helps me return to my heart when I get too much in my head. He says, "Valentina, you are not in your heart." Sometimes I fight him and say, "Yes I am." To which he replies, "No, you are not. If you were, you would not say those things." When I want to be an emotional disaster, I just am. Then, when I feel like I can't go on anymore, God sends loved ones to give me hope. So I stay alive for those I love. After some time, my soul starts finding reasons to live again, things that make me happy.

Ironically, my son taught me more about happiness after his death than when he was alive. When he died, I had to move into that bigger world to find him. When I did, I realized that all our loved ones, all those who come from God, are there. They are always connected to us, giving us encouragement and support.

For example, I once treated a blind man from India who came to see me with his wife. While they were waiting, his wife noticed pictures on my wall of Indian President Giani Zail Singh and me that had been taken when I was doing some healing work with him When I came out to greet them, the man told me that he had been the President's doctor and that the President had been assassinated a couple of months earlier. In that moment, we knew that the President had guided them to me after his departure from this world. This story shows that our connections with our loved ones are never over.

My friend Misha and I have this same type of connection with Yogi Bhajan, whom I first met in Moscow in 1990 at the Global Forum on Environment and Development for the Survival of Humanity. When he was living in America, we went to visit him many times. Now that he has passed away, we still see him. We'll walk down the street and pass by a Sikh wearing a turban and we'll know it is Yogi Bhajan saying, "Hello, guys, I'm here." He always had such an amazing sense of humor.

Q. How do you balance planning with remaining open to opportunity?

A. I keep track of my appointments. But other than that, I like to keep my schedule flexible so I can go wherever I am needed. For example, some years ago I met H.H. Sant Rajinder Singh Ji Maharaj, an internationally known Indian Spiritual Leader. This meeting happened at an international forum created by another very special person named H.H. Acharya Sushil Kumar ji Maharaj (Guruji), founder of the World Fellowship of Religions. Sant Rajinder Singh, a head of Sawan Kirpal Ruhani Mission/Science of Spirituality, was the president of the Seventh World Religions Conference in 199Q. That's where I met him the first time. When I returned to India in 2000, I wanted to find him but I did not know where to look. One night, my Russian friend and I were eating at a French restaurant in Delhi and I was telling him about Rajinder Singh. Right when

I was saying how much I wanted to find him, Rajinder Singh walked into the restaurant. My friend's jaw dropped and he said to me, "Valentina, do you realize that you have been talking to me in English for some time?" And my friend did not speak English.

We continued eating and I kept thinking about whether I should talk to Rajinder Singh or not. I finally decided not to and when we were leaving the restaurant, we passed right by his table. In fact, we had to, there was no other way to the door. Something stopped me right in front of Rajinder Singh's chair and I started talking to him. I told him that I had met him at the forum and had wanted to find him but didn't know how. As his people were giving me his schedule and contact information, he said to me, "So that's why I am here. I usually don't go for dinners like this and wondered why I'd come." The people at his table were shocked that he was saying this to me. It was not the kind of thing he normally said.

How can you plan a meeting like that? There is no way. People plan their lives for years and then God comes in and changes everything. Some people experience that change as hardship. I'm not saying people shouldn't plan. I'm just saying they should build in extra time so they have the freedom to pursue the opportunities that life brings.

Q. If you received $100,000, how would you spend it?
A. I would spend the money just as I do now—on giving my husband and me time to travel, meet people, and write about them. All around the world, people are just waiting to tell their stories. Their life stories are our greatest spiritual teachings. Actually, my husband is saying that we wouldn't even need to write a book or do healing work. We could just travel around and let people see us so they would know love exists. That's all any of us really need to know. When my hus-

band and I are in airports, people often stare at us (especially teenagers) because of our love for each other. So we would use the money to travel and share love. We'd also use it to help people do the things they want to do.

Q. If you had thirty seconds with someone in an elevator, what three things would you tell the person to do to be joyful, peaceful, and whole?

A. I would look into the person's eyes and start talking to him or her. Their eyes would give me the words I need to say. I'd say the words that would help the person open to life and the healing that is there. For example, I recently met a truck driver in Russia who was planning to go to Magadan, a town in far east Russia where Stalin used to keep prisoners. The depth of the man's eyes was amazing. Just by looking into them, I knew what to say.

Sometimes people cross our paths for a reason but we won't know what that reason is unless we look into their eyes and stay open to the experience. When we're open, then we become joyful, peaceful, and whole too. For instance, when I was flying back to America, I asked to change my seat for one in the middle. The woman at the ticket counter stared at me in disbelief saying, "Are you sure you want a middle seat?" I replied, "Yes, I'm sure." But given her reaction, I thought I must have done something wrong. Maybe the flight was full and I would be squished.

However, when I walked onto the plane, I saw why I'd asked to change my seat. Sitting next to me was a Catholic monk who was born in America but had been living in Magadan for fifteen years. He had written two books about people who were prisoners there under Stalin's oppression. For his research, he had interviewed over five hundred of them (only two hundred are still alive). He now was working on his third book about the prisoners' children. I knew God was telling me, "Valentina, there are places like Magadan that you didn't think about visiting. But would you consider it?" Of course I would. I want to go where I am most needed. There are people all over the world whose eyes I want to look into, even for only thirty seconds in an elevator.

Q. What books or resources have helped you the most? Why?
A. When I was a teenager, my spiritual teachers were artists such as Michelangelo, Leonardo da Vinci, van Gogh, Mozart, Chopin, and so on. I would read about their lives and they would teach me about God, even though I didn't believe in him yet. For example, I read that van Gogh painted with coffee when he didn't have colors. What greater spiritual teaching is there than someone making the impossible, possible? So I would point to people who overcame incredible odds to share their gifts, their art.

My husband and I are collecting movies and books about people with inspirational lives. For example, we recently saw the film *La Vie En Rose* about French singer Édith Piaf. She was in pain all her life and even had trouble walking. But somehow she got the whole world to listen to her sing. I had the chance to share her story when I was teaching at an orphanage in Russia. I said to the children, "Do you believe in miracles?" They replied, "No, we don't." So I said, "I do." They asked, "What kind of miracles?" I told them I was watching a movie about a girl who couldn't see. The prostitutes who lived with her prayed to a saint to restore her sight and she saw again. I said that girl grew up to be the world famous singer Édith Piaf. I know these children will remember this story and believe that miracles are possible. I certainly will because I find people's life stories to be the best inspiration.

Native Americans often say that we are going through a time of change and that our ancestors are coming to help us. To connect with all the people that came before us, I go onto the Internet to learn about them, see their faces, and hear their voices through their art and poetry. This reminds me that they are always here supporting us. We just need to ask for their help.

Q. What would you like to be written on your tombstone?
A. "Love is what to remember." I want people to remember me with love. After my son died, I thought about writing a letter to my friends and family, which they could read after I die. In it, I would say, "I will always love you. I will always be there for you." When I first came to America, I thought I was here to teach people about herbology and healing. Now I know that I came to teach and learn about love and freedom. So I want people to remember that love is in everything. And that love and freedom are their birthright from God. My memory is important only if it helps those I knew remember this more easily.

Q. Anything else?
A. The year my son was sick, I experienced love from him that I didn't know existed in the human world. He would look at me, smile and say, "Mom," and I would feel so much love. Once you have love, it just grows and grows and you have to keep sharing it because what else can you do? To survive, you have to give it to the world.

This book you are writing will help people discover their love and inner freedom. It will open them the way God has opened me.

"Sometimes being on the edge allows greatness to come through."
Tamara Bowman Mooers, President, Emerald Echo, the Resort. Author, *Living on the Edge of Goodbye* and *Emerald Echo-The Story*

Tamara Bowman Mooers is committed to awakening authentic self-expression and uncovering the hidden treasures that lie within us. As a licensed psychotherapist, Tamara shows us where we get stuck in relationships and how to transcend the internal walls that prevent us from experiencing intimacy with others and ourselves. For fifteen years, Tamara successfully worked with abused children, adults, and couples. As a professor of human sexuality at Orange Coast College in Costa Mesa, California, thousands of students report that her entertaining style of addressing sensitive, sexual topics has transformed their lives. Tamara is known as the "sexpert" on international LA Talk Radio. As an inspirational speaker and workshop trainer, Tamara brings a wealth of experience in love, loss, ancient wisdom, and humor that will give you a new awareness of what is possible for your life.

Tamara is the founder of Emerald Echo, a world-class entertainment and wellness resort offering transformational workshops, peace talks, a day spa, art gallery, and dolphin-assisted therapy. She is the author of two books, *Living on the Edge of Goodbye . . . A Story of Hope, Healing, and Encouragement after Betrayal* and *Emerald Echo—The Story*, a children's book. In addition, she is a contributing author to the Amazon number one bestseller, *Law of Business Attraction*, by Ruby Yeah.

Q. What experiences put you on your spiritual path?
A. Before coming into this life, I believed there were certain

experiences I needed to have, in order to become who I was meant to be. Some of these experiences were painful and abusive. During the deepest, darkest night of my soul, I cried out to God asking, "Why the depths of this pain?" A still small voice came back and said, "Tamara, forgive me." I replied, "What do you mean forgive you? I have been asking *you* to forgive *me* my whole life." The answer came back, "I'm sorry for what you have gone through. It was all necessary for what I have called you to do. You had to experience extreme pain to gain the depth of understanding."

Q. How did these experiences change you?
A. They kept breaking up the illusions around me. I was born into a family that valued image. Everything was about how you looked and came across. Internally, the masks and walls were breaking apart until there were only broken pieces left inside. Through my healing, a mosaic masterpiece formed from my broken pieces. God's light is now able to shine through those shattered pieces, allowing a prism of colored light to pour out of my heart. The light coming through my broken pieces is more powerful than any clear-cut perfection.

One of these experiences was when my former husband got on the Internet and decided to rekindle a romantic love affair with his old high school prom queen. When this happened, I felt a crack inside my heart like a lightning bolt splitting me in two. I cried from the core of my being, "God, this is too painful. How will I ever survive? Please take my life." When God didn't, I said, "If you're not going to take my life, then please send me angels. Show me my purpose for being here now. If I'm going to stay, then help me really live! I don't want a mediocre life anymore. That's a death in itself. Please give me a word, because I can't hear scripture being quoted by well-intended people trying to comfort me."

I felt God say, "Tamara, millions of people have been through this before you, and millions will go through this after you. What's going to make your experience any different?" When God conveyed this, I came to a place of surrender, and then another awareness broke through. I said, "God, give me the mind of Christ . . . even as Judas gave Jesus the kiss of betrayal, Jesus still loved him. Give me that kind of heart."

The love I had come to know rose up inside me, and I was able to leave my former husband in love. When I confronted him, I said, "I love you enough to want what you think is best for you, even if it's not me. So make your plans to be with her." When I released him, I felt free to be who God called me to be—with a knowing that one day I would be in love again, this time with someone who matches my mission here on Earth. My former husband did me a favor! He had the guts to leave what wasn't working for our highest good.

A year later, my social work job was coming to an end. My last day would be February fourteenth, Valentine's Day. I asked God, "Is this really it? Am I to walk away from my secure income and retirement?" I felt God say, "Tamara, on February fourteenth, will you marry me?" I replied, "Yes, I'm yours." As I grieved and let go to soar off the cliff, God caught me in his hands. I felt like an eagle waiting for the wind of Spirit to take me higher and higher.

In living from this space, I've found it's rare to come across other eagles. There are many canaries who are perfectly content to stay perched at the end of a branch talking about the latest gossip. And it's not that eagles don't like canaries, they do like them. They just don't have time for idle chitchat. Eagles love to soar and live at greater heights. So when I do come across another eagle, I feel a squeal of excitement. It's so powerful to be with others who have chosen to live from the "inside out" versus the "outside in."

It's like the golden Buddha that was covered up in clay. The clay is all the crap that happens to us. We get buried in judgments like, "You're not good enough. You don't matter." People are afraid to go underneath because they think they're going to find more crap. What's really there is gold—pure love and light that embraces us.

My gift is speaking the truth in love to let others know that everything is as it's supposed to be. So when pain comes knocking at your door, open it and say, "Oh, you are here again." Let the pain in, and do not allow it to leave without giving you a gift. It's like thrusting an icicle into your heart. What happens when ice meets heat? It has to melt. Your pain will never stay as acute as first felt. It has to change form. The pain gives you an opportunity to ask, "In light of this challenge, who do I get to be now?"

Q. What changes are you noticing about your life and the world?
A. When you change the way you see the world, the world changes. I asked God to let me see people the way he sees them, no matter how buried their light. With those eyes, I fall in love with everyone I meet. It is a pure kind of love, one that's different from the sacred intimacy I share with my partner.

Really, the biggest change is knowing that life is about what I love, not what loves me back. We must give the love that's inside us, regardless of whether people give it back. My first children's book was about being able to deal with illness, bullies, mean teachers, parental divorces, and so on. The second one is about giving kids scenarios in which they can expand in love when someone shows up spewing venom.

How beautiful it is when we can be angry and still say, "I love you," knowing that we are creating it all. There are no villains and victims. Everything is happening for us and by us. Everyone is just a mirror allowing our souls to become bigger.

Q. What changes are others noticing about you?

A. I've become hilarious as I have gotten really honest about embracing myself. So when somebody says, "You're crazy," I reply, "I know. Sometimes it really serves me!" The other day, someone tried to corner me by saying, "Hey bitch, are you for real?" My first reaction was, "Uh oh!" Then I put my hands on my hips and said, "Thank you for noticing. It serves me well." It was interesting to watch her mood shift as she turned around and laughed. She knew she was not going to get a rise out of me. If we are truly all of it—the light and the dark—then, as author Debbie Ford says, we can put a cover plate on ourselves so nobody can get under our skin. I have learned to laugh at myself instead of letting others pick at the parts I don't want to own. In turn, I totally accept them. Without judgment, everyone gets to be who they are. Literally, you can fart in my presence and it's fine. Go ahead. I'm just kidding!

Q. What has been the most challenging part of your path?

A. The most challenging part has been to embrace all of me. We teach what we most need to learn. So everything I'm telling you, I'm saying to myself. It's like, *Girlfriend, where are you not loving yourself?* because there are so many parts of me that I want to beat myself up about. Then I think, *That really makes me sad*. As I connect to God, I realize that I receive his love by giving it out. As I extend it out, it reflects back to me. So my challenge is not to isolate myself because part of me wants to protect and pull in. While the cave of solitude shelters me, it also brings me great sadness when it's a prolonged experience.

Q. What is your earliest memory? Why do you remember it?

A. I was just on a cruise with Louise Hay, Brian Weiss, Iyanla Vanzant, Wayne Dyer, Gregg Braden, and Cheryl Richardson. Being in the presence of these people was like coming home. Brian Weiss took us back through our childhood and past lives. When he took us to our earliest childhood memory, I remembered being at Disneyland between the Haunted House and Mark Twain's theme boat. I felt the awe of being at Disneyland. And I remember loving that space between those two theme park rides and feeling that life could be like Disneyland—scary and adventuresome.

In my life, I have gone through haunted valleys of pain. However, I always felt my soul pulling me forward saying, *It's okay, Tamara. You will live through this. Look at what's available on the other side.* Knowing that adventure was possible encouraged me to imagine Emerald Echo, the resort. I have wanted to create this place since my earliest childhood memory. That reminds me of a quote by Mark Twain: "Forgiveness is the fragrance that the violet sheds on the heel that has crushed it." That's what I've done with my life. I've turned darkness into the fragrance of beauty.

Q. Who are your mentors? What have you learned from them?
A. Neale Donald Walsch and his book *Conversations with God*. One of the best experiences of my life was being able to share my journal writings with him. I said, "Neale, the way you ask God questions and the way God answers you back, that's the way I've been journal writing for years." We had such camaraderie when I shared my writings with him. Neale felt like a colleague who is both divine and human. My experience with him helped me realize that God can use me too.

Another inspirational mentor was renowned psychotherapist Virginia Satir. Satir was all about the experiential aspect of therapy. The root meaning of the word psychology is "to bring up one's soul." Satir got that and transformed people's lives through interventions like "The Parts Party." I experienced a beautiful example of that kind of work at Debbie Ford's Shadow Process workshop. She really helped me embrace my darkness, as well as my light. I have all my clients read her book, *The Dark Side of the Light Chasers* as well as Walsch's *Conversations with God*.

Greg Mooers of LifeCamp also inspires me. He took me through a process that helped me identify my "heart virtues," the virtues I would give my life for. My heart virtues are unconditional acceptance, self-worth, and personal freedom. These virtues helped me see exactly who God created me to be. Now there is nothing to attack or defend—only truth. When we live in truth, the world looks different. As *A Course In Miracles* says, "Nothing real can be threatened. Nothing unreal exists. Therein lies the peace of God."

Another mentor is Louise Hay, founder of Hay House. She is all about self-worth. She says, "What you think about is what comes about." I marvel in her conviction and in her ability to walk her talk. When I met her on the cruise, I said, "Louise, I have loved you forever. Thank you for how you have shown up." She looked at me in a nurturing grandmother way and said, "Tamara, that's wonderful." Her mirroring back to me the beauty I saw in her was really powerful.

I also love Wayne Dyer. On that same cruise, I would walk by him and say, "Hello Wayne," and he'd say, "Hey Tamara." That was precious. I also connected with Cheryl Richardson. I love her authenticity in expressing how afraid she is sometimes. Being able to share our challenges around extreme self-care makes it easier to transcend them. As Walsch says, "What's in your best interest is also in the other person's best interest." Being able to say, "No, that doesn't work for me," helps people, because when you do say, "Yes," you mean it.

Q. What is the greatest challenge facing society?
A. Getting past the illusion, the density that appears so real. When you look at the density with your five senses, you cannot see the light. Yet the sun is still there even when clouds cover it. It's about living as the indigo and autistic children do. They come into life with enormous gifts that see beyond our knowingness. Dolphins also have this higher intelligence. With their sonar, they read our hearts and help us heal

whatever is not in alignment. Often, when these things are physical, they are considered handicaps. But they may not be because some of the happiest people I know are mentally challenged. As Forrest Gump said, "Life is like a box of chocolates. You never know what you're going to get." These children have happiness that transcends the minutia we try to analytically pick apart and wade through. The first half of my life, I tried to study what made relationships work. Then I got to a place where I let all that go. Because on the other side is surrendering to what is. There, everything is perfect. It's exactly as it's supposed to be.

Q. What advice would you give someone just starting his or her spiritual path?

A. When clients come to me, they are afraid. So I like to disarm the atmosphere by saying, "You can verbally vomit with me and it's okay. None of it is gross." One of the analogies I like to use is, "You know how beautiful it is to sit on the beach and watch the ocean waves? Well, it's a whole other experience to put on a scuba suit and dive into the water. There are some scary things underneath the surface. But there are also treasures. That's what being with me is going to be like. We'll put on our wet suits and dive in together. Know that I will be with you and we'll go only as fast and as deep as you are ready. I'm willing to go to the darkest places with you because I know what's available on the other side. I will be pulling you forward where the light awaits."

Recently, I finished writing a children's book called *Emerald Echo—The Story*. It explores the universal truths of forgiveness and freedom and is my gift back to all the abused kids I have worked with over the years. One of the things I used to ask them was, "What's the best thing that could come from being abused?" At first, they were taken aback. Then they would say, "Well, I guess it made me stronger." It's even deeper than that. They get to choose to use the experience to expand their hearts or to close down and become perpetrators. I used to tell them, "Be angry. Do what you need to do. But at some point, recognize that your traumas never have to equal who you are. Use your hurt to discover the light inside you. You have a choice to become exceptionally compassionate."

Q. What are your practices for connecting to your higher purpose?
A. Gratitude. I wake up in the morning, take a breath, and give thanks for everything I have. Then I meditate by sitting in the presence of God. He is always there, but I especially feel him when I am observing my breath during meditation and when I am reading *A Course in Miracles*. My number one connection to God is through journal writing. It's sometimes difficult for me to sit still, so if I keep my hand busy, I get quiet more easily. Then I can be a conduit for the words that come through. I start writing and say, "Father, I am here," and he talks to me.

One of the names God has given me is, "My angel of mercy." I love mercy. It's beyond grace. He so lovingly reminds me that he's with me and everything is okay. He also prepares me for what's ahead. I just close my eyes and God shows up in an indigo color that floods my awareness. When he shows up in my mind's eye, I lie down and am suspended in space as I gaze upon the Trinity. Then I feel lightning bolts of electricity fusing every cell of my being. And I ask God to let me be a conduit of his love, to let me get out of the way so people can feel him when they are near this garage—this body—I've parked my soul in. Because that's all my body is: temporary housing around my eternal soul.

I tell abused kids that no matter what happens to our bodies, a part of us always remains unscathed. That part is whole, perfect, and complete. And what happens to our bodies is just an opportunity to allow our souls to show up even bigger. When I get them to see that, true healing occurs. When I extend that to someone else, then it also happens for me. I am so grateful to give it, because it is what my soul longs for.

Q. How do you use these practices when you get out of balance?

A. I get honest about how I feel. I say, "God, it really hurts right now. What's the purpose of this? Please enlighten me." I go into this deep inquiry and ask God to bring a sign or someone who can show me what I'm missing. Sometimes I hold on to the pain for a couple of days, allowing it to go through me like shrapnel. Like that icicle thrust into my heart, I let the pain in so it can melt and flow out. Then I'm free to have more light come in. In the past, I used to get stuck in, "Why me?" Now, I look at it like, "Okay, it's here. What's next? There has to be more."

Recently I said to God, "If you love me like I think you do, let that show up in the form of a male partner who reflects the relationship I have with you." What's so cool is that it did. I am experiencing a depth of healing and love like I've never known before, except with God. This kind of love I'm experiencing now is so beautiful that I could die today knowing that all was well with my soul. It's like crossing over the desert to the land of milk and honey. My prayer was, "God, if my life is meant to be in the desert and I have your presence, I can do that. But if there is a way that we can do the land of milk and honey with your presence, I'm all for it." Now that it's come, I feel truly alive. It's juicy and intoxicating.

Q. How do you balance planning with remaining open to opportunity?

A. I never would have believed it possible to accomplish what I have this past year and a half. My prayer is, "God, just light enough for the next step," because if I looked at every task I had to do, I would just lie down and take a nap! So I prefer to give up the how and eat the elephant one bite at a time. In the past, I mostly accomplished things on my own. If I could have done Emerald Echo that way, it already would have come to fruition. But God knows I need a team of people working with me who believe in bringing heaven on Earth.

So I'm welcoming a collaborative team of unexpected opportunity. "Stay open, who knows, lightening could strike." That's a line from the movie, *Meet Joe Black*.

I got a profound lesson in staying open to team support when I was at T. Harv Eker's Enlightened Warrior Camp. In the seminar, we had to carry bricks up to the top of a mountain. I remember feeling heavy and burdened thinking, *This is my life. I have to carry everything alone.* Then a man came up behind me and said, "Ma'am, can I help you with one of those bricks?" I almost broke down and started sobbing. For someone to come along and help me carry the load validated that I don't have to do everything by myself. Then the man said, "Is there anything else I can do?" I replied, "Actually, yes. If you can take my hand so I can feel I'm with someone, then I can know I can do this."

We made it to the top of the mountain. Right then, I knew that the difference between making it to the top and not making it was who I'm partnered with. Being in partnership with someone who shares the same mission of uplifting the planet is so exciting. It's like pop rocks going off in my mouth.

Q. If you received $100,000, how would you spend it?
A. I would use it to move Emerald Echo's team forward. The entire plan is in place—the executives, the property, and so on. We're like a rocket ready to launch and the $100,000 would be our fuel to take off. God has called me to remind people who they are: whole, perfect, and complete. To have a place where people can come and experience this is what the money would do. At our facility, they will be held in the heart of God, where they will forever be at peace.

Q. If you had thirty seconds with someone in an elevator, what three things would you tell the person to do to be joyful, peaceful, and whole?
A. If the person seemed troubled, I would say, "Hi. I'm sensing you might be going through something. Is there anything

you'd like to share?" Then I'd create space for the person to just be. When someone experiences unconditional acceptance, they are free to let go of whatever holds them from the light. If I can help create the space for their light to emerge, then that's what I'd do for them.

Q. What books or resources have helped you the most? Why?

A. The number one resource is journal writing. It helps me listen to my inner voice. I drown out every other voice and go within to speak to God. It's great to look outside for inspiration, but it's even greater to be inspired from within. If we don't go within, we go without. So create a journal to tap into your inner guidance. It will help your unique gifts emerge. The truth is that we are all special, whatever our gifts or perceived handicaps. It's all part of revealing the light that we are, the part of us that is changeless, the part that already knows that all is well with our souls. And whatever happens outside will pass.

Q. How do you resolve the paradox that we are already everything we seek yet we still have a mission to fulfill on Earth?

A. There is a knowing of our place in this world and there is the mission to fulfill. And I've come to believe that balance is overrated. Sometimes being on the edge allows for greatness to come through. I sometimes work all night because God has called me to do something. I complete it without any qualms. I do, however, sleep until ten o'clock the next morning. As long as I've exhausted everything God has called me to do, then I know I've done my part. It's when we get caught up in saying, "It's mine," that our grasping prevents us from realizing our dreams. It used to be like that for me. Emerald Echo was my baby and I was afraid to share it because I thought somebody would steal it.

The truth is that Emerald Echo is God's dream in me. Now, as I build it, I surrender it back to him because it doesn't matter who comes along and picks up the next piece. I know that my part was played out in full. I can truly rest in that. I can say, "God, I followed your guidance, sometimes with resistance, but I always listened to your voice." Letting it go allows the opportunity to flow.

Q. What do you think of the concept that my enemy is my lover?

A. I like it because there is no separation between enemy and lover. It's like Neale Donald Walsch's book, *The Little Soul and the Sun*. In the last line of the book, God says, "Remember, I have sent you nothing but angels." So the people we consider enemies are not. They have agreed to dim their lights low so we may know ourselves as the special gift we came to experience. This collaboration between enemy and lover helps us be the presence of God.

Q. What would you like to be written on your tombstone?

A. I like going to funerals because they remind me of how I want to live. My manicurist recently asked, "Tamara, what do you want people to say about you at your funeral?" I replied, "I want someone to say, 'Tamara loved with all her heart. She held nothing back. Her candle was burned out completely.'" To look down on my funeral and have someone say that would validate my life's purpose—that I kept filling up with God and pouring back out.

Q. Anything else?

A. We come into this world yearning to know God and fulfill our purpose. It's like starting out at the bottom of a mountain, trying to get to the top, where God is. As we climb higher and higher, we see everything more clearly. We realize that despite our different semantics and religions, we are all saying the same thing. We are all one. When we get that, we could never imagine harming others, because hurting them would mean hurting ourselves. The closer we are to God, the more we realize we are all of it: the light and the dark, the perpetrator and the victim. In that place of peace, we don't need to be right. We just get to love.

"All that we are arises with our thoughts. With our thoughts, we make the world."

-Buddha

"The world is an illusion. Enjoy the ride!"
Chad Cameron, Leap! Ventures LLC

Prior to making the "Leap" into filmmaking and seminar teaching, Chad was an entrepreneur operating a computer consulting company in northern Colorado. In 2005, Chad watched the documentary *What the Bleep Do We Know!?* The science discussed in the film provided the piece Chad needed to understand how quantum mechanics influence daily life. This understanding sparked his awakening and cocreation of *Leap! The Movie* with Isaac Allen (www.leapmovie.com). Chad has found his niche: teaching, coaching, and filmmaking. He enjoys helping people grow through understanding philosophical concepts. The key to it all is choosing a way to look at life's challenges that leaves you empowered.

Q. What experiences put you on your spiritual path?
A. In 2001, I went through a divorce. I realized there was a possibility that some of it was my fault and I didn't want it to happen again. At the time, I thought it was ten percent my fault, which seems silly now. I view this as a pivotal moment because until I took some responsibility, I was trapped. Taking responsibility was the first step and I sought counseling. My counselor recommended I watch the movie, *What the Bleep Do We Know!?*. The film made sense to my scientific mind and I began seeking answers.

I then found myself in a series of personal growth seminars, met my business partner Isaac Allen, and read Robert Scheinfeld's book, *Busting Loose from the Money Game*. In his book, Scheinfeld states that money—and the world—are an illusion. In reading these words, I realized I was like Mario in the video game and all I had "to do" was let go and surrender to "what is." My first step toward freedom was to understand that I was trapped in an illusion and needed to wake up. I now see that the entire world exists in my consciousness. There is nothing outside of me.

Q. How did these experiences change you?
A, I'm both Mario in the video game and the programmer who designed it. As the programmer, I decided to jump into the game and have my awareness shift from the programmer's perspective to that of Mario, the character in the game. With this awareness shift, it is easy to get sucked into the drama of being Mario and judge events as good or bad. When I return my awareness to that of the programmer, I realize I create everything in the game: my divorce, father's death, and car crash. From this viewpoint, it is easy to see the perfection in everything. It is only when I have Mario's perception that "problems" exist.

Q. What has been the most challenging part of your path?
A. What's a challenge? Now that I understand I create everything—from the programmer's perspective—and that it is all scripted, there are no challenges. For example, during the filming of *Leap!*, both my father and dogs died. These were not "fun" experiences from Mario's viewpoint. However, the more I return to the programmer's perspective, the more I remove judgment and problems dissipate.

Q. What changes are you noticing about your life and the world?
A. I believe the world is an illusion and the changes I see "out there" reflect what is going on inside me. Before creating *Leap!*, I was in relationships that didn't serve me. As I changed, these relationships gracefully fell away and new supportive ones emerged. Many things in my life have shifted similarly.

Q. What changes are others noticing about you?
A. I'm a lot more fun. My bookkeeper, a friend for almost a de-

cade, says I rarely get upset. When something goes wrong, I realize it's all part of the script and my distress quickly dissipates.

Q. What is your earliest memory? Why do you remember it?
A. When VCRs came out, my sister and I were very young. One day we were at the junior high where our Dad taught science and managed the audio-visual department. He set up a camera and VCR and videotaped us. When he played the tape back, I thought we had gone into the TV. I remember asking the following week, "When can we go inside the TV again?" Obviously, we hadn't gone into the TV, but now I see my question reflected assumptions. As Mario in the video game, I may think I know what's going on but, in reality, nothing happens as it seems. It is only when I zoom out to the programmer's perspective that I get an idea of what is really going on.

Q. Who are your mentors? What have you learned from them?
A. Will Arntz, the creator of *What the Bleep Do We Know!?*. His movie did me a great service by getting me to realize that physics and spirituality are really the same thing in two different languages. Robert Scheinfeld and his book, *Busting Loose from the Money Game*, which got me to see that life is an illusion I created so I could play in it. Then there is Jed McKenna. When you are ready to play spiritual hardball, pull out one of his books. He pulls no punches and tells it like it is.

Q. What is the biggest challenge facing society?
A. Where I sit, the whole thing is an illusion. It's like asking a dreamer what's the biggest issue he faced in his dream. To give you an answer, I would say we each have a choice to wake up or not. This is the only challenge I see.

Q. What advice would you give someone just starting his or her spiritual path?
A. All the non-dualistic traditions emphasize the same truth:

There is no separation between divinity and us. So start with what speaks to you. There are so many great resources out there. I can talk about my experience and what has worked for me. Watch supportive movies like *Leap!* and *What the Bleep!?*. Read Arnold Patent's *The Journey* and Jed McKenna's *Spiritual Enlightenment: The Damnedest Thing*. *A Course in Miracles* is a great place to start. Gary Rendard's *The Disappearance of the Universe* is contemporary and fun.

Q. What are your practices for connecting to your higher purpose?

A. I return to the awareness that I am the programmer. I remind myself that I put on the skin suit known as Chad so I can play the game in a world of limitations. These limitations, or rules, make the game more fun, just as they do in sports or video games. What fun would it be if I could create whatever I wanted, if my team got a touchdown every time? So my practice is to connect to who I really am by remembering that when things aren't going my way, from the skin suit's perspective, I let go of how I think they should be. When I do, it's funny how everything works out perfectly in the end.

Q. How do you use these practices when you get out of balance?

A. I recognize that I'm the programmer and that I wrote the code for everything that is happening. It's sometimes hard for the Mario (the Chad skin suit) in the video game to see this perfection, like when my dad died. When I, the skin suit, can just be with the experience and get that I, the programmer, created it, then I can remove any judgments and be at peace. Once I understood this, the grief and sorrow around my father's death dissipated and I opened to joy and appreciation. Now I realize I am my father. He and I are of the same code, the same programmer—just in different skin suits. We're like aspen trees that look separate above ground but share the same root system. Where does one aspen tree start and another end?

Q. How do you balance planning with remaining open to opportunity?

A. Life is an unexpected opportunity and I "plan" as little as possible. I plan only events like trips and meetings that involve others. My life is lived from inspiration. People and resources just show up when needed. When I live from this context, everything seems to work out. Nothing appears that isn't programmed; your video game won't end until it's done.

Q. If you received $100,000, how would you spend it?

A. I would do what I was inspired to do in the moment. If you handed me $100,000 right now, I would use it to make multiple documentaries quickly by outsourcing most of the work. We have lots of ideas and money would make them come to life even faster.

Q. If you had thirty seconds with someone in an elevator, what three things would you tell the person to do to be joyful, peaceful, and whole?

A. 1. Watch the movie, *Leap!*. It shows the commonality among different spiritual paths.

2. Adopt the attitude of seniors who let things go without getting their feathers ruffled.

3. Understand you are the player in a video game and you created it to have experiences. Realize that the most important thing in life is to have fun.

Q. What books or resources have helped you the most? Why?

A. Everything I encountered during the making of *Leap!*. *Leap!* was an amazing part of my journey, filled with heart wrenching growth and transformation and incredible peace and joy. In the film, we've taken Eastern philosophy and made it accessible through using modern language and analogies to help people wake up from the dream. Other resources include (books) Arnold Patent's, *The Journey, Spiritual En-*

lightenment: The Damnedest Thing, by Jed McKenna, and *A Course in Miracles*, by Helen Shucman and William Thetford.

Q. What would you like to be written on your tombstone?
A. As any non-dualist would tell you, in the end, it really doesn't matter. I view life as a video game and once my game is over, it's over. There is nothing "out there," which includes tombstones. But to play along with your question I would say, "The world is an illusion. Enjoy the ride now!"

Q. Anything else?
A. I recently visited a butterfly sanctuary and saw an important parallel to our spiritual journey. The spiritual journey is like a butterfly's life cycle. We are born and enter into life as larvae. During the caterpillar stage, we get to crawl around in the muck of drama. Then something traumatic or insightful happens and we start to awaken. This is the cocoon stage, where we begin undoing the caterpillar programming. Typically, these experiences are not fun from the caterpillar's perspective—what I affectionately refer to as the "getting your butt kicked" stage. After we have matured, we awaken, emerging from the cocoon literally transformed. Caterpillars often ask what it's like to be a butterfly. Until they've entered the cocoon, they are not able to hear the answer. I love what Richard Bach says: "What the caterpillar calls the end of the world, the Master calls the butterfly."

"Be Christ on Earth, here and now."
Pamela Chapman, iAscend Programs, LLC

Pamela Chapman is a life strategist and motivational teacher who helps women expand beyond perceived limitations to raise the bar on their lives. She uses cutting edge coaching techniques to enhance women's self-esteem and launch them into their God given purpose. Prior to becoming a strategist, Pamela served in corporate America for over twenty-nine years. Pamela holds a degree in programming from Orange Coast College, Costa Mesa, California, and is a Certified Coach. She also is a Certified Domestic Violence Specialist, a Certified NAMI Mental Wellness Specialist, and a Certified Drug and Alcohol Awareness Specialist. She has won numerous public service awards and is a published author. Pamela has one son, five grandchildren, and an eighty-six-year-old mother with whom she now lives.

Q. What experiences put you on your spiritual path?
A. My parents joined the Pentecostal church when I was eight to help heal our family from violence. When I was eighteen, I left the church because I didn't want to serve a vengeful God who would send me to hell if I didn't do what he wanted. When I turned thirty-five, I was sick and tired of being sick and tired and started my personal spiritual search.

Q. How did these experiences change you?
A. When I returned to God, I was on the verge of a nervous breakdown. I went to Crossroads Community Church in California, and one of the ministers said, "Someone has come today with lung pain seeking answers." My left lung had collapsed a few weeks earlier so I felt like he was talking directly to me. The church's pastor, Chuck Kruse, introduced me to a loving God, one who met me where I was. Through Christ, I improved my life. I quit drinking, smoking, and became a

better mother to my son.

Q. What has been the most challenging part of your path?
A. Trying to experience God's love in the strict Pentecostal faith. All I ever heard was, "No you can't do this. No you can't do that." People are bound to fail on this path because no one can follow all the rules. I didn't want to serve a God that was all about restrictions and condemnation. Fortunately, I found a loving God through Pastor Chuck Kruse, Bishop Clarence McClendon, and Dr. William Hinn.

Q. What changes are you noticing about your life and the world?
A. Putting God first gives me freedom and liberty. God gives me a love for people and life. I now believe that heaven and hell are states of being. Heaven is knowing that Christ lives in me—I'm his hands, mouth, and feet. I don't necessarily believe in organized religion because people often use it to control others. People resent Christians who proselytize and try to convert them. I'd rather be Christ's love in the world, sharing his passion and freedom with everyone I encounter.

Q. What changes are others noticing about you?
A. One friend said, "You're so full of light. You're my angel in the darkness." People often say I'm a giver, fun to be around because I'm filled with joy and life. I'm positive, finding the good in everything and everyone.

Q. What is your earliest memory? Why do you remember it?
A. When I was about seven or eight, I asked my father for my weekly two dollar allowance. He replied, "You're just a two dollar whore." Those words stay with a girl forever. I've written a book called *Heaven's Hell: The Beginning*. In the novel, I dramatize the effects of domestic violence on a young girl's life, showing the emotional and psychological damage it can cause.

Q. Who are your mentors? What have you learned from them?

A. My eighty-six-year-old mother Louise, who taught me strength and perseverance. My high school gym teacher, Mrs. Collins, who made me proud to be an African-American woman. Also, my college music teacher, who asked me to play a piano piece for my final exam. When I sat down on the bench, I froze. She said to me, "I don't know what's happened in your life but you're an incredible woman. You already have an 'A' in this class. You can do this. Now, play!" I played it beautifully. From these women, I learned self-esteem. Now, as a coach, I help other women build their confidence.

Q. What is the biggest challenge facing society?
A. America has become a nation of greed. We worship money as our god. We need to return to the basic values of God, family, and the golden rule, "Do unto others as you would have others do unto you." Right now we are lovesick for President Obama because he brings a message of hope. However, it's not just up to Obama. We all need to serve humankind.

Q. What advice would you give someone just starting his or her spiritual path?
A. Look inside. The answers are within you. Find a loving pastor or spiritual leader who can help guide you. Join a spiritual group, one that supports you. Remember, you are the temple with your own unique spiritual path.

Q. What are your practices for connecting to your higher purpose?
A. In the morning, I meditate and pray for God's guidance. I feel his presence and listen to the direction he wants me to go. When I was in that place of devastation—losing my husband, quitting my job, and moving to Colorado—I retreated, taking time to heal, rest, and wait for God's direction. I felt God in me so powerfully but I also felt my husband, and he was pulling me to the grave. My body started shutting down but my will to live was stronger. I cried out, saying to my husband, "I love you but I can't come with you." Then I committed my-

self to life. I returned to California every two months to see Dr. Diane, my nutritionist, and Dr. William Hinn, my pastor. I repeated to myself, over and over again, "I am health, the healed of the Lord. Christ died so I could be whole." I was transformed by the renewing of my mind, daily. Out of this grief and redemption, iAscend Programs was birthed.

Q. How do you use these practices when you get out of balance?

A. When I get out of balance, I quiet myself, meditate, and pray, returning to my centeredness in Christ. This practice helps me let go. I also laugh with friends and talk with my coach, Debbie Scott. I teach similar practices to my clients. We all need practices because life is what it is and often will throw us challenges.

Q. How do you balance planning with remaining open to opportunity?

A. When I worked in corporate, I got upset when things arose that changed my plans. Now life has taught me to go with the flow. I write a plan but then go with the day. God will upset my plans anyway as he guides me to what he has for me. If it feels right, I just do it.

Q. If you received $100,000, how would you spend it?

A. I'd donate fifty percent to my nonprofit for ending domestic violence and use the rest to take a trip to Hawaii with my beau, do something nice for my mom, promote my business, and send a love offering to Dr. Hinn.

Q. If you had thirty seconds with someone in an elevator, what three things would you tell the person to do to be joyful, peaceful, and whole?

A. I've personally made Christ number one in my life. I live in the present and try to just be. It takes the pressure off of life. I listen to the voice inside because it always guides me down the right path.

Q. What books or resources have helped you the most? Why?
A. The number one best seller of all time, the Bible. *The Game of Life*, by Florence Scovel Shinn and *Secrets of the Millionaire Mind*, by T. Harv Eker. I also appreciate Christian and gospel music and the teachings of Dr. William Hinn. One of my favorite Dr. Hinn teaching series is *The Future's Past is Now*. In studying this series, I came to fully understand living in the now. I do get off the path, but now quickly self-correct when I worry about the future or things I cannot control.

Q. What would you like to be written on your tombstone?
A. "A woman who loved life and loved to love."

Q. Anything else?
A. Live life and live it more abundantly. Cherish every moment because, as 9/11 showed us, we can get raptured up at any moment. Be Christ on Earth, here and now. Continue the work he began and remember, "Where sin abounds, [his] grace abounds even more." (Romans 5:20)

"Om Mani Padme Hum
The Jewel in the Heart of the Lotus!"

-Mantra of Avalokiteshvara

"Everyone is the Buddha."
Jason Chen, Chinese Intuitive and Fortune-Teller

Jason Chen is an intuitive and fortune-teller, originally from Taiwan. He moved to the United States when he was a teenager. He has master's degrees in business and finance and currently works for the State of Colorado as an information systems manager. He also teaches computer courses at Metropolitan State College and the University of Denver. He lives near Denver with his wife and two children.

Q. What experiences put you on your spiritual path?
A. When I was in seventh grade, I took up photography and bought a lot of equipment. Then my father lost his business, so I had to find a less expensive hobby. I always liked mystical things, so I thought, *Maybe I'll do fortune-telling*. I began reading books on the subject and tried to find a master to follow. All the masters I contacted said, "You are only fourteen. You are way too young to start this career." Since no master would teach me, I started learning directly from books. The first book was the *I Ching* that taught basic concepts such as *Ba gua*, yin and yang, and the five elements. It was fascinating, but I had a hard time exciting others about it. So I expanded into face and palm reading. I bought very few books. I mostly stayed in the bookstore and studied there. Even though I was failing my school courses, I could read a fortune-telling book once or twice and have it memorized.

After business hours, people would come into the bookstore and I would approach them and do readings. I examined people's hands and faces and asked them questions about what had happened in their lives. Their responses would clarify what I was seeing and I was about eighty to ninety percent accurate. I also did birthday calculations called *Zi Wei Dou*

Shu, which we now have software for because they take a lot of time to compute by hand. The bookstore patrons would say, "Why are you doing this? You are such a young kid. You can't possibly understand these deep concepts." Despite my young age, they listened to me and became my first clients.

When I left Taiwan and came to Colorado, I would go to a friend's restaurant and do intuitive readings and fortune-telling there. My guy friends wanted to learn how to read palms so they could hold girls' hands. I thought, *That's not the right motivation*. Some of my clients read fortune-telling books and try to do it themselves, but it's not that easy to apply. It takes a lot of practice as well as knowledge of how to combine different symbols. In Taiwan, books discuss why people with the same name or birthday have different faces. Fortune-telling is scientific. It is good to collect multiple data points like hand, face, birthday, name, and feng shui. Then you can see a more complete picture of each person.

In China, we believe one-third of your fate is based on timing, one-third is based on resources, and one-third is based on free will. I always give people a positive way to look at things. There is no good or bad fate. It is based only on your point of view. That's the major difference between Eastern and Western philosophy. The West is more absolute and the East is more relative. For example, China takes a more nuanced position on North Korea and Iran, whereas America says you are either my friend or you are my enemy.

I am very accurate when I say the first thing that comes to mind. When I hesitate, I'm not as accurate. I don't do intuitive readings or fortune-telling for people I know because they are too familiar and I cannot sense them as strongly.

Q. How did these experiences change you?
A. I learned there is no world out there. There are no other people. There is only me. All this was created to test me. Every-

one is the Buddha. Even the guy pointing the gun at me is a Buddha. So when I change my thoughts, the world changes. We have to believe that whatever is happening right now is the best thing that can happen. If a genie appeared and said, "I can take you back to any time in your life but after, you will forget I was here," then we would have to believe that life is giving us the best possible journey. There is no need to feel unsafe or to ask for more. When you gaze upon the Buddha, you don't ask for five million dollars. You think, *Wow, he did it. By doing less—nothing or no thing—he gave a lot to everyone.* If you celebrate this in him, then you will look on the bright side in your own life and be happy with what you have. For example, I was unemployed for five years. Without that time, I probably wouldn't have married my wife, had my kids, and focused on my family. I believe that was a lesson I had to learn before I could step up to the next level.

Q. What changes are you noticing about your life and the world?
A. When I started doing intuitive readings and fortune-telling, I became more courageous. I saw people more deeply and had greater awareness of the Earth and environment. It also increased my interest in studying different religions. I read about Buddhism, Taoism, Christianity, and Mormonism. I haven't studied Islam yet, but I'd like to.

Q. What changes are others noticing about you?
A. My parents didn't believe I could do fortune-telling until they came to the Dragon Boat Festival, where I was doing intuitive readings. Then they heard people say how good I was and started to think I might know something.

Q. What has been the most challenging part of your path?
A. I get tired at big festivals where I look at over one hundred hands a day. Even when my energy and vocabulary run low, I still carefully select my words, especially if there is a big crowd gathered around. Another challenging yet rewarding part is seeing people touched by my work. A few years

ago, a beautiful young Vietnamese woman and her friends came over to see me. I kept avoiding talking about her life line because it was very short. She kept asking me about it and I said that the quality of life was more important than the quantity. She pressed me for a number and I said she would live to forty-five, even though my feeling was really thirty-five. Later, a guy came over and said I had talked to his girlfriend. I said, "Which girl? I have seen so many today." He replied, "The one you told would live to forty-five." I inquired, "What did she think of that?" He said, "Great. The doctor said she wouldn't live past thirty-five." My hair stood on end. Sometimes I scare myself.

Q. What is your earliest memory? Why do you remember it?
A. When I was three years old, I wasn't walking very well. I remember my sister holding me and I was so afraid she would drop me. I also remember crying for an hour when my mom put me on a desktop so she could cook for her friends. I cried because I was afraid that if I moved, I would fall off the desk. I had this same experience when my mother was folding clothes and put me on the bed, where I could not move around. Overall, I had very slow growth as a child until I came to the U.S., where I grew very fast, possibly due to the hormones in the beef! The Chinese believe that fortune-tellers have extra abilities that other people do not have. When I look back, I see that this is true.

Q. Who are your mentors? What have you learned from them?
A. I never did find a teacher so I am self-taught. The more intuitive readings I do, the better I get. It's kind of like being a doctor. Physicians learn through practice, through their internships, residences, and years of seeing patients. I don't like studying, but I seem to learn best from books and practice as evidenced by my two master's degrees.

I knew one other person who did fortune-telling. I met him through a student organization. He died very young, at age thirty-two, so he never had the chance to read my fortune. He had a very special method of reading people's hands—from the backside instead of the palm. It would have been great if he could have read my fate. I would have been like a doctor who got sick and had to see another doctor.

Q. What is the greatest challenge facing society?
A. Accepting people's differences to a certain degree. The question is: To what degree? We have to keep practicing tolerance and fine-tuning it. In Eastern culture, we believe in discipline. When I was in school in Taiwan, we all sat face forward and listened to the teacher. We were supposed to absorb information and not ask questions. Even if our parents were wrong, they were never wrong. Our society encouraged everyone to be the same. In America, we cherish individuality, courage, and heroism. Here respect goes both ways, even between parent and child. It's kind of hard for me because I was educated in both places and am caught in the middle. But being in the U.S. has helped me see the importance of diversity as well as the need to unify around something. That's the balance we need to find.

Q. What advice would you give someone just starting his or her spiritual path?
A. In special situations, I share my own story. There was a girl who came to me wanting to take care of her parents. She worried about how much money she could make so she could give it to them. I told her, "I feel your parents. They want you to shine. If they see that, they will be proud. Don't worry about the money. It will come. Just focus on shining." Then I told her when I first came to the U.S., I failed most of my classes, especially English. So I wasn't looking to stay here. One day my sister said, "Why don't you remain in the U.S. for a year? Your English will improve." While staying with her, I ate dinner at nearby Chinese restaurants. Five nights in a row, I got fortune cookies that said things like, "You are at the turning point of your life," "You are at the crossroads

of your destiny," and "From now on, your life will be so different." I thought it was a message so I decided to stay here.

A few days later, my father asked, "Do you want to stay in the U.S.?" I replied, "Sure." He was surprised because I had not wanted to stay before due to my poor English. Then my dad took me for a walk. On the walk, he told me that he'd never had a complete family and that true happiness came from keeping the family together. He was crying and I felt sad, too, but I said, "Dad, if I go back to Taiwan, I will never face my fate. So regardless of how much the apple wants to stay in the tree, when its time comes, it must drop to the ground." After some minutes, my dad said, "Okay. Let's go inside. I'll teach you how to wash your dishes and clothes." I told that girl my story to show her that sometimes we need to be strong. Our parents will understand and be proud.

I don't share other people's stories because that would violate client confidentiality. So as soon as I read someone's fortune, I immediately forget it. This keeps me clean.

Q. What are your practices for connecting to your higher purpose?
A. When I first learned fortune-telling, I would practice by reading people's faces as I walked down the street. This helped me get faster and more accurate. Eventually, I no longer had to push myself because doing readings just came naturally. When I was in Taiwan, I used to do calligraphy and recite sacred texts, which helped me grow spiritually.

Q. How do you use these practices when you get out of balance?
A. I sometimes get mad, but I bring myself back quickly. I do this by stepping back and viewing things from a different angle. Once you have adversity in your life, then nothing really gets to you. When I was a kid, I never received good grades and sometimes got beat up by bullies. In the U.S., studying be-

came even harder because my English was so bad. I also was unemployed for five years but that time was important because it changed my mind-set. Without a job title and money to prove my worth, I eventually realized that I am who I am. Now I take things easier and do what I can to help people. With adversity, you see life from a larger perspective.

Q. How do you balance planning with remaining open to opportunity?

A. I work for the state and have a fixed schedule, so I don't plan as much as I did when I was on my own as a financial advisor. When I was in graduate school, I had a ten-year plan that I kept updating, which detailed how much money I would make and save by a certain age. After I got laid off, I was not that organized anymore. Now my focus is my kids. I plan my schedule around them. Being home those years I was unemployed really changed me.

Q. If you received $100,000, how would you spend it?

A. Could it be one hundred million? It might not be enough for something really big. I would put some in the bank and use some for a down payment on an investment property. I plan to retire at age fifty-five. My dad said, "Why do you want to retire so early? You will die sooner." I replied, "The reason I work for the state is so I can retire in mid-life with seventy-five percent of my income as pension. Then I can return to Taiwan and take care of you." He liked that answer. I also tell my children, "When you grow up and have kids, I will live nearby and take care of them. I will take them traveling across the country in my recreational vehicle."

Q. If you had thirty seconds with someone in an elevator, what three things would you tell the person to do to be joyful, peaceful, and whole?

A. Do less. I used to do more and more and finally let it go. What's hard now is helping my kids do less. My son, for example, has piano lessons, swimming lessons, and two after school enhancement programs for English and math. He is very busy. I feel sorry for him.

Q. What books or resources have helped you the most? Why?

A. I like to spend time outdoors with friends camping and fishing. I sit out in the boat just waiting for the fish to bite and think, *Wow, this is the life*. So my advice is to find an outdoor place that relaxes and cleanses you. For example, people often put crystals and rocks in their homes to purify the energy. Periodically they need to bring these crystals out into nature to clean them. We too are like crystals that need to go out into nature to get clean. When we die, we should choose a burial spot that is the right channel for our energy. This will help us prepare for our next life.

Q. What would you like to be written on your tombstone?

A. In China, we say that a tiger is supposed to leave its fur and a man is supposed to leave his name. Usually only very famous people are remembered. My children and grandchildren will remember me for a while and then I will fade away. Dr. Morrell, one of my professors, inspired me to teach. If I can teach ten or thirty years and have just one or two students' lives change because of me, then my life will have been worth it.

Q. Anything else?

A. Recently, I started telling my clients to take better care of themselves. I said to one woman, "Treat yourself like your daughter. Would you let your daughter go to bed late or eat bad food?" She replied, "No! You're right. If I treat myself like my daughter, I will be a lot better off!"

"Know God's intense love for you."
Father Tom Coyte, Priest, Holy Cross Catholic Church

Father Tom Coyte is the Pastor of Holy Cross Catholic Church in Thornton, Colorado. Father Coyte has been a priest for thirty-five years and has served at Holy Cross for the last twenty. Father Coyte has been involved with deaf ministry since he was in the seminary. Holy Cross has over 2,000 members, 250 of which are part of the deaf community.

Q. What experiences put you on your spiritual path?
A. I was born into an Irish Catholic family, on my mother's side, and attended Catholic school. That was the beginning of it. My faith was strong. I never really questioned it. While in high school, I signed up to do Perpetual Adoration at church late Friday nights. That brought me closer to God. Later, I went to Notre Dame and there made the decision to go to seminary.

About three years before I was ordained, the archbishop visited the seminary and mentioned the need for someone to do deaf ministry. I wrote and said I was interested. I don't know exactly why. Some might say the Holy Spirit. I began working with the deaf, took sign classes, and got deeper and deeper involved with deaf ministry. One thing led to another.

Q. How did these experiences change you?
A. One blessing for someone who goes into the priesthood is seminary. It was a great time. For seven years, I got lots of education and formation. It was a chance to explore my relationship with God and what I really believe. I think the priesthood is a good match in terms of my personality, skills, and what I love to do. The biggest changes came in terms of growing up and maturing. Developing self-confidence and

self-love, too. I was trying to figure out who I was and that didn't happen until my mid-thirties, several years after I was ordained.

The reasons I became a priest are not the reasons I stay a priest. I initially was attracted to the priesthood because of a desire to serve God and others, and also because it seemed like a safe place to go. There was a certain immaturity or lack of self-confidence in me, especially in terms of relationships. Over the past twenty-five years, I have grown up and am able to relate better to people. So the reasons I stay a priest are almost the opposite of what they were in the beginning. I came in to run away and I find myself now drawing even closer.

Q. What changes are you noticing about your life and the world?
A. Priesthood is very flexible, so you can paint a picture of a job that fits who you are. As I have come out of my shell, I have been able to be more of a leader as a priest and pastor. This has changed how I see the church and my role within it.

My dad had a profound impact on how I see things. He wasn't Catholic. He was a lawyer and a judge who had the ability to see both sides of an issue. I think all my family members are like that. We are not judgmental. We are more curious about why people do what they do. This has been a great blessing in my life. It leads to more humility in terms of who people are, who I am, and who God is.

Q. What changes are others noticing about you?
A. My lifelong friends see in me more confidence, more outgoingness, and more of an ability to take charge. I had been one of those students in school who never said anything. It would scare me to death to raise my hand. I was very much an introvert. Still am. And part of the journey has been to change that. I think I have succeeded. But I have worked at it. You set a goal and you can do it.

Q. What has been the most challenging part of your path?
A. Growing up and being honest with myself. Also, the work of the parish presents different challenges at different times. Each time I get a new task, I've got to really develop my skills. By personality, I am a big picture person, not a detail person. I'm interested in getting projects started, but once they are, I lose interest. In a sense, that's good because my job is to get things going and have others do them. But at the same time, I don't want to do that to a fault. So I've got to be concerned, lend support, and make sure things work. It's been a challenge to pay attention to detail, to not live down the road but live in the now.

Q. What is your earliest memory? Why do you remember it?
A. I remember my family moving when I was three years old. It was a time of real change for us. We had been living in Fort Collins, Colorado and then bought a small farm north of town. I recall how old I was because I have memories of our house in town, as well as those out on the farm.

Q. Who are your mentors? What have you learned from them?
A. My family members were mentors. They were strong, good, loving, and caring. My mother's Irish Catholic side passed down the faith. My father's mountain rancher side passed down a strong work ethic. Growing up, some teachers at Catholic school were mentors. Also, some seminary professors because of who they were and their witnessing to me in their spiritual journeys. Through the years, I have had some good friends that have helped me in this whole process of self-discovery.

Probably the key changing moment in my life occurred in my early thirties. One day I was bemoaning whatever was going on at the time and taking my usual introverted stance. Then I realized how stupid it was and I had the deepest belly laugh. I had always assumed that whomever I was with would rather be with somebody else. This made me very uncomfortable and that's what I was laughing at. That realization transformed my life, slowly but surely.

Q. What is the greatest challenge facing society?
A. Peace with justice. More and more, I see the need to take risks and speak out on behalf of the Lord's peace—as opposed to the world's peace. Injustice abounds. It's never ending. But to commit oneself to working for peace with justice is critical. I believe that Christianity, especially Catholicism, has so much to offer the world in its search for values because we preach the power of love—sacrificial love—and I don't know that anybody else really does. Love your enemies. It seems to be a uniquely Christian message and one that does not even span all Christian churches. The challenge is preaching the gospel and being faithful to it. Finding ways of sharing it, not in the sense of forcing someone to go to church, but in the sense of seeing the wisdom of Jesus. To me, that gives life meaning. It's something worth dying for. Not that I want to just yet.

Q. What advice would you give someone just starting his or her spiritual path?
A. I would try to really listen and get to know who they are. We are all so delightfully unique. A lot of those questions you have been asking me, I'm sure everybody answers them differently. And they must to be true to themselves and not embrace a religion or practice for the wrong reasons. That's where my dad's influence comes back into my life. I wouldn't automatically hand someone a rosary and tell them to pray. Of course, I want them to know the joys, depths, and riches of the Catholic tradition. But at the same time, it has to be true to where they are coming from.

I'll share a story that comes to mind. I had a man who was a Buddhist, but had grown up Catholic, come to me wanting to get back to the church and communion. I asked him why. After a lengthy discussion, it turned out it was because of his mother. That's not a reason to do it. He was very happy as a Buddhist. And now he is a good friend. But he is not Catholic.

Q. What are your practices for connecting to your higher purpose?

A. I like quiet time. I don't try to fill it with a lot of words. I'm trying to get away from that when I am in the presence of God. I do enjoy the scriptures. Daily Mass is such a blessing because I have to prepare a homily every day. I also spend a lot of time during the week working on sermons. It gives me a chance to explore the scriptures and develop a deeper understanding and appreciation of the riches there. I do some spiritual reading, more periodicals than books. I'm not a big reader. Even if authors have only one idea, their books have to be this long in order to sell [uses fingers to show one inch]. So I think, *Why do I have to read a whole book for that one idea?* I am better with reference books and that sort of thing.

Q. How do you use these practices when you get out of balance?

A. I don't have a violent temper. As I mentioned, I am not quick to judge but am more curious about why people do what they do. So if somebody cuts me off in traffic, curiosity is more my response. I do get angry sometimes. I have learned to laugh at myself when I do and then back off. I don't often act out of anger. And undoubtedly to a fault because there are times when we need to act out. For example, I preached this morning about injustice. When someone is doing something unjust, we need to call him or her on it.

Q. How do you balance planning with remaining open to opportunity?

A. I'm a planner. I work hard at my calendar trying to get the priorities organized. Once a month, I sit down with my goals and objectives and look at my progress. At the same time, a lot of things just come up as part of being a priest. If people die or get sick, I drop everything and take care of them. I have worked a lot on time management and am learning how to put things in proper perspective.

Q. If you received $100,000, how would you spend it?
A. One of the things that has always appealed to me is the Campaign for Human Development. That kind of work is so crucial because it builds structures that get at the root causes of poverty and injustice instead of just throwing money at the problem. I would set up a fund to support such projects. The fund would help me keep some control so the money would go to good use. I'd also probably buy a new car.

Q. If you had thirty seconds with someone in an elevator, what three things would you tell the person to do to be joyful, peaceful, and whole?
A. Know God's intense love for you. Make sure you love yourself. That's the only truth. Everything else either agrees with that or is a lie.

Q. What books or resources have helped you the most? Why?
A. I'd say the first resource is the church—meaning the community or "little church." Having people in your life that love and support you is so vital. I have found the scriptures to be a great resource although they can be difficult at first. It takes a bit of foundation work, so I recommend classes such as our small faith sharing communities. Once you build a foundation, the scriptures open up and there is so much there. If people are readers, I recommend finding good spiritual texts as opposed to the stuff that's usually more available. If somebody's not a reader, then there are classes, CDs, and DVDs.

Q. What would you like to be written on your tombstone?
A. I don't really care. My will says I'll be buried in the priests' plot at Mount Olivet. I would like to be cremated because it seems silly to be buried in a body with all the expenses involved. What people say about me is not a biggie in my

life. When I was ordained, I had a holy card that said, "When through one man's life, a little more love, a little more compassion, a little more caring comes into the world, then that man's life has meaning." I guess I'd still hang with that.

Q. Anything else?
A. Don't just take what society offers in terms of religious or spiritual teachings because there is a lot of junk out there. You can spend too much time watching television evangelists who have to preach something that puts enough money in the collection plate to keep going. This includes our dear Mother Angelica on EWTN. So be cautious about what's good and what's not. One of the things that is very big in America is fundamentalism. Fundamentalism is about power and control, not about belief and authentic worship. And whether that fundamentalism is Bible or church based, it's still about power and control and it's still not healthy.

You might want to ask the fundamentalists you interview, "Where is the darkness? Where is your greatest sorrow and anxiety?" When people are so controlled by thoughts of the devil, it can be frustrating. They live in a magic world over which they have no control. Sometimes I want to shake them out of it. And then I laugh at myself.

Q. What do you think of the concept that my enemy is my lover?
A. When I saw the movie, *The Secret*, I thought it was total selfishness. It was like what you see in television advertisements. Get the money or the woman. Jesus was wise in saying that this kind of stuff is false joy. Real joy is loving your enemies. That type of sacrificial love is what Christianity and Catholicism offer.

"Great ideas originate in the muscles."

-Thomas A. Edison

"I explore the world with my eyes shut."
Ann Cunningham, Sculptor, Multi-Sensory Artist, and Author

Ann Cunningham has been a sculptor for more than forty years. Her work is featured in numerous public and private collections such as The Denver Art Museum, The Museum of Outdoor Arts, the Colorado School for the Deaf and the Blind, and the conventions of the National Federation of the Blind. Ever since she can recall, Ann has expressed herself through art. Although she has years of experience in various art forms, sculpting remains her passion. She loves working with archetypal imagery—myths, fairy tales, and dreams—because it promotes dialog and shared experience among diverse peoples. She creates pieces that engage the viewer's mind and heart, fostering a sense of connection, mystery, and excitement. Sculpting, exhibiting, and teaching have given her the opportunity to see things from different perspectives. Her work with the deaf and blind communities has given her a whole new world to explore, one filled with subtle nuance that enriches her conscious and subconscious minds with images that she wouldn't have been able to understand otherwise.

Q. What experiences put you on your spiritual path?
A. I connect to spirit through my artwork. Art has been a constant thread throughout my life. For many years, I searched for a way to contribute through art but had trouble finding it. Process art seemed limiting because it did not take me beyond myself. Then one day I stopped at an intersection and thought, *I need to get clarity or I'll be stuck here*. After that realization I quit drinking and started showing my art in public. While hanging a picture for a Naropa exhibit, I asked, "Could someone who is blind understand this picture?" This inquiry lead to my creating a show called By Touch Alone in which blind and sighted artists from around the country

exhibited their work. As I displayed a blind artist's piece—warped cardboard that I pulled out of a dilapidated box—I questioned whether it was acceptable art. Then I remembered to close my eyes and feel the work. It immediately transported me to the beach in a way that was more powerful than any picture I'd ever seen. In that moment, I knew my purpose was to create multi-sensory art.

Q. How did these experiences change you?
A. I found my purpose. I am a translator of visual images for the blind and a multi-sensory artist who creates works that can be appreciated by all. David Hockney, in his book, *Secret Knowledge*, contends that art, and the world, became more vision-centric with the advent of the camera obscura and mirrors at the start of the Renaissance. The photographic style of painting that came from these inventions was in sharp contrast to earlier medieval works such as *Saint George and the Dragon*. When you see this piece, you can tell the artist was feeling it, not just seeing it. Fast-forward to the invention of the printing press and Internet and you realize that most of our information is visual. Even textbooks are fifty percent pictures, and these images are not translated into Braille or audiotapes for blind readers.

That's where I come in. My teaching and artwork help translate these images for the visually impaired. For example, I show my blind students how train tracks come together in the distance by having them stand in two parallel lines. Then I have one student at the front use her hands to track their voices to the back of the class until her palms touch. This experience demonstrates that a translated picture really is worth a thousand words.

Q. What changes are you noticing about your life and the world?
A. I get to explore the world with my eyes shut. As I do this, I realize that what I thought was visual is really not. For example, scientists recently did a study in which they put sighted

participants under sleep shades and had them learn tactile skills such as Braille. Within three weeks, their tactile sensory functions reverted to the visual part of the brain. If I had an MRI, I bet my brain would show the same phenomenon. We have the opportunity to create a new art form, one of seeing pictures with our hands. When we feel artwork, it comes alive. I originally created a piece called *Five Ravens*, which I renamed to *Animated Raven* after feeling it as one bird jumping into different positions instead of the five birds I originally had intended.

Q. What changes are others noticing about you?
A. My family thinks I'm on an unusual path but they are proud of me and trust my judgment. My daughter's friend recently had concerns about adopting a blind cat. My daughter said to her, "Really? There's no problem with being blind." Her positive attitude shows how all our lives have been touched by this work.

Q. What has been the most challenging part of your path?
A. Finding what I was called to do. I was in my forties when my interest in tactile/visual art first peaked at the Naropa exhibit. And I fully committed to this path when I turned forty-eight. Now I am pioneering a field outside the bounds of traditional art. It's exhilarating and I feel very fortunate to be contributing in this way.

Q. What is your earliest memory? Why do you remember it?
A. When I was six months old, I crawled across our sofa to get a pull toy. When I reached it, my brother said, "You win!" and pulled it away from me. I started to cry. It's traumatic to be told you have won when you have really lost. My older daughter uses similar ruses to get her way with the younger one. This subterfuge may be a common experience for children and adults.

Q. Who are your mentors? What have you learned from them?

A. My art is my primary mentor. I spend hours in the studio, which is my own perfect world. My parents and daughters are mentors. My mother taught me creativity, my father taught me kindness, and my daughters taught me focus, perseverance, and forgiveness. Tu and Lane Saan Moonwalker, Native American authors and light workers, have also been an incredible spiritual influence in my life.

Tu and Lane Saan Moonwalker recently wrote a book called *Business Revolution Through Ancestral Wisdom*. In it, they show how the universe flows in a circle. When our activities flow in this manner, we receive incredible support from the cosmos. So aligning with this flow can help us create lasting peace and happiness. It can also help us restructure our businesses so they continually receive energy to remain vital, sustainable, and prosperous. I carry this wisdom into my art. It feeds me spiritually.

Q. What is the greatest challenge facing society?
A. There isn't one. We are living in extraordinary times and are doing exactly what we need to do. In his book, *Voices of the First Day: Awakening in the Aboriginal Dreamtime*, Robert Lawlor describes a 70,000 year cycle split into two time periods: the matriarchal and patriarchal. In the matriarchal time, the seed germinates, the flower blooms, and the fruit sets. In the patriarchal time, the time we are living in, the fruit grows and ripens and gets ready to drop to begin the cycle again. This dropped fruit can either smother or nourish the seed. Our excess consumerism is the rotting fruit smothering us a bit. However, we will find nourishment because we have many more cycles to go.

Q. What advice would you give someone just starting his or her spiritual path?
A. No one is just starting his or her spiritual path. You can make your journey more satisfying by discovering who you are and what you want to contribute. Books such as *The Artist's Way*,

by Julia Cameron, can help. You can also join a group to support you in finding your purpose. Last spring, I joined a focus group to examine and recommit to my art career path. In the group, I depicted where I wanted my art to go. Since then, my art has gone through the roof. Give yourself the time to stop, focus, and vision what it is you wish to create.

Q. What are your spiritual practices for connecting to your higher purpose?

A. I stay connected to my body through exercises and offerings I do each morning. Being fully present in these practices helps me make headway. My primary spiritual practice is art. I love spending time in my studio sculpting pieces in a quiet, meditative state. However, as with all life, art is best seen in the reflection of others. So I encourage myself to get out and share it, especially with my students.

Q. How do you use these practices when you get out of balance?

A. I recently felt disappointed when my proposal for selling a public art piece was rejected. After figuring out what I could do better, my disappointment faded. I now have a clear picture of where to go from here. This shift in attitude is in contrast to my early life when even the smallest criticism would send me into despair. For example, one of my art teachers criticized my work and I didn't paint for two years. I have come a long way.

Q. How do you balance planning with remaining open to opportunity?

A. I hang a chart on my wall that lists all my projects and serves as a visual reminder of my next steps and deadlines. Knowing where I am in relation to these milestones helps keep things loose. Sometimes I enjoy completing a long list of tasks. Other times, I spend the whole day sculpting. I never set a time limit on my sculptures because I want them to be the very best they can be. That said, I always see ways to improve them. Perhaps this is just part of being an artist.

Q. If you received $100,000, how would you spend it?
A. I would buy land with a water supply on which to build a house, grow my own food, and live debt free. I plan to do this anyway, so if you increased the sum to one million, I would invest it in my art. The extra money would free up time for more sculpting. However, I don't know whether my artwork would really improve. The impositions I experience help keep me real.

Q. If you had thirty seconds with someone in an elevator, what three things would you tell the person to do to be joyful, peaceful, and whole?
A. I would ask, "What is it that you love to do? How does it serve others? Find out and focus on that."

Q. What books or resources have helped you the most? Why?
A. The best books on multi-sensory art are:
- *Art Beyond Sight: A Resource Guide to Art, Creativity, and Visual Impairment*, by Elisabeth Salzhauer Axel and Nina Sobol Levent
- *Art History Through Touch and Sound: A Multisensory Guide for the Blind and Visually Impaired. The Building Blocks of Art* (book 1) and *European Modernism: 1900-1940* (book 2), by Art Education for the Blind, Paula L. Gerson and Elizabeth Salzhauer Axel.

While these books offer a wealth of information, they focus mainly on research, not art. I prefer to spend time collaborating with visually impaired artists to create new works. As we develop more material, we will find new things to investigate. On a different note, when I am sculpting, I enjoy listening to books on tape, especially ones on the government or art. If I need to concentrate, I turn them off and work in silence.

Q. What would you like to be written on your tombstone?
A. I want to be flayed on a Tibetan cliff side and have the birds eat my remains. I would like to be remembered as the grandmother of tactile art. I have seen myself as a grandmother since age five and would derive satisfaction from knowing I shared with people how to see the world in a new way.

Q. Anything else?
A. If you tell me it can't be done, I will do it. That's the kind of person I am and that's what attracted me to doing multi-sensory art. I am a pioneer in a field with a paucity of work so there is always more to do. I like the challenge of creating this innovative art form.

"It is! It exists! All that is or was or will ever be is right here in this moment! Now!"

-Peter Matthiessen

From THE SNOW LEOPARD by Peter Matthiessen, copyright © 1978 by Peter Matthiessen. Used by permission of Viking Penguin, a division of Penguin Group (USA) Inc.

"Life only happens now."
Hale Dwoskin, The Sedona Method

Hale Dwoskin is the author of the *New York Times* best seller, *The Sedona Method: Your Key to Lasting Happiness, Success, Peace and Emotional Well-being*. Hale is one of the teachers from the movie *The Secret* and a founding member of the Transformational Leadership Council. He is the CEO and director of training of Sedona Training Associates, an educational organization headquartered in Sedona, Arizona. He cofounded the company in 1996 to teach courses based on the emotional releasing techniques originated by his mentor, Lester Levenson. Hale Dwoskin is an international speaker and featured faculty member at Esalen and the Omega Institute. For over thirty years, he has been teaching The Sedona Method to individuals and corporations throughout North America, Europe, and Asia and leading facilitator trainings and advanced retreats since the early 1990s. He is also the coauthor with Lester Levenson of *Happiness Is Free: And Its Easier than You Think* (a five-book series).

Q. What experiences put you on your spiritual path?
A. I'm not really sure. There was no defining experience that said, *Okay now I'm on my spiritual path*. I was drawn to spirituality as a teenager. The first thing I did was read a couple of books—*Autobiography of a Yogi* by Paramahansa Yogananda and *The Story of Edgar Cayce: There Is a River* by Thomas Sugrue. That was in 1970 when I was about eighteen. Spirituality was what I was most interested in and that has never changed.

Q. How did these experiences change you?
A. The limits I thought I had started falling away. Then everything began accelerating when I met my mentor Lester Lev-

enson. Up until then, I was doing a lot of different things—reading books, attending seminars, and practicing tai chi and yoga. Meeting Lester focused my spiritual path on The Sedona Method. With it, I immediately began feeling profound shifts in awareness. I started getting glimpses of oneness and feeling more peaceful and at ease. I also got the bug to share this process with other people. That bug—that desire to help others through The Sedona Method—continues to this day.

Q. What has been the most challenging part of your path?
A. Staying with working on myself. There are times when I want to give up. I get sick of examining my own navel. There is only so much lint I can take out! So, off and on, I hit walls of resistance. But nothing has ever really dissuaded me.

Q. What changes are you noticing about your life and the world?
A. As I kept seeking, I began feeling more peaceful, happy, and alive. Then in the mid-1990s, I started having awakening experiences. At some point the experiences stopped and there was just this steady knowing of the truth of who I was. I don't really buy into any sense of limitation the mind throws up. It hasn't stopped doing that. I just don't buy into the drama for very long—usually seconds, sometimes minutes. There's just a constant state of happiness, joy, and peace no matter what the body-mind is experiencing, even through things that are intense like health, business, and relationship challenges. Over time these things have less ability to disturb this body-mind in any way.

Q. What changes are others noticing about you?
A. Lester must have seen something in me because he insisted I take the copyrights to The Sedona Method. I initially protested. I thought some nonprofit should take them over. People close to me now notice a greater sense of imperturbability. I'm not disturbed by what's going on around me. I'm happier, more peaceful, and easier to be with. I also have greater interest in the well-being of others and the planet.

Q. What is your earliest memory? Why do you remember it?

A. When I was still processing, I used to remember traumatic things from my childhood. But all those things have lost their sting. The first thing that comes to mind is summers at camp. I lived in New York City, so going out into nature really made an impression on me. Looking back, I realize that when I was outdoors, my mind was quiet and I was in love with the moment. Now, I don't need to be in nature to do that, but back then I did. Watching the sunset or seeing a fish in the pond helped me be with what is.

Q. Who are your mentors? What have you learned from them?

A. Lester Levenson. He was the first person who said to me, "The only thing you have no choice about is the fact that you are already whole, complete, and perfect as you are." I was angry at him for saying this because I didn't see it that way. But as I persisted, I discovered that he was speaking the truth—not just about me, but about everyone. Through knowing Lester I learned it was possible to feel unconditional love for another human being. I don't know why it was so. I guess it was just the resonance we had for each other. That unconditional love changed the path of my life. It's why I gave up my six-figure income and moved out to Arizona to work with him in 1987.

Q. What is the greatest challenge facing society?

A. On one level, what's here now is always perfect, even when we can't see it. When we look back on our lives, for example, we realize the things we thought were bad were often our greatest gifts. On the human level, I'm hoping that's the case with our planet because unless we start living sustainably and treating each other as brothers and sisters, the Earth won't survive in its current form. What's encouraging is that there is a small minority of people waking up to the truth of who they are. And they are taking responsibility for creating positive change. But it's still a small minority. Most people continue to live only for themselves as though they are separate—as though the world is their enemy and something to be consumed. But I'm encouraged because the movie *Letting Go* is helping The Sedona Method reach a broader audience. There are other positive things, too, that are starting to counter this trend. I just hope it's not too little, too late.

Q. What advice would you give someone just starting his or her spiritual path?
A. There is no path. What you are seeking you already are. Instead of going off looking for a path, just notice what's already here. If you start exploring what's here now, you'll find that the now has lots of answers, lots of possibilities of self-discovery. You can discover that you are not separate. You are not an individual who needs to seek. The presence of awareness that gives life to this moment is who you are.

Q. What are your practices for connecting to your higher purpose?
A. When I let go, I get clearer and clearer about what the right thing to do is in the moment. I become more at ease with what is. I'm okay whether or not I achieve my goals. It's very liberating and, at the same time, it makes it much easier to achieve because I see what my highest and best purpose is right here, right now. The other thing that happens is I care more about others. I don't just live for myself. I care about the planet and the people around me, whether or not they oppose me. This is my experience and the experience of thousands of people I have worked with over the past thirty years.

Q. How do you use these practices when you get out of balance?
A. I don't do much processing anymore. It usually happens spontaneously. If I do process, I simply allow what is to be. For example, if my wife Amy and I are having an argument, I allow it to be. Then it passes and we find resolution. When I was younger, I used to fight against life. But that fight has just

about disappeared. It still comes up from time to time but it doesn't last very long.

Q. How do you balance planning with remaining open to opportunity?
A. Without some planning things wouldn't work. If I didn't plan retreats, for instance, people couldn't come. Just know that God/Goddess is laughing whenever you plan because things don't always turn out as you expect. So planning is a natural part of life. It's just that we take our plans way too seriously.

Q. If you received $100,000, how would you spend it?
A. I'd spend it helping get this message out to the world. I'm watching what's happening as people see the film *Letting Go*. It's not quite as powerful as taking a Sedona Method seminar or reading the book, but it's profoundly changing people. As the movie gets into mass consciousness, I think it will make a huge difference to the planet.

Q. If you had thirty seconds with someone in an elevator, what three things would you tell the person to do to be joyful, peaceful, and whole?
A. I wouldn't use words. I would just love them as they are. Because in thirty seconds anything I'd say would just be white noise. But genuine love and care is enough to change the energetic.

Q. What books or resources have helped you the most? Why?
A. I would recommend the movie *Letting Go* and the book *The Sedona Method*. Eckhart Tolle's books are very helpful too. We see eye to eye on most things. The only difference is I give more of a practical "how to." I also like some of the current Advaita teachers like Sailor Bob Adamson, John Wheeler, Francis Lucille, and Tony Parsons. If you are going to read a book, read one about non-dual reality.

Q. What do you enjoy most about supporting people with The

Sedona Method?

A. It's really wonderful to see the profound effect this process has on people. To watch them as they shed their suffering and discover the truth of who they are. It's part of why I work so hard. The other thing I find really satisfying is being able to point to the truth. It's a conundrum, really, because I can't speak the truth, but I can point to it. I like pointing people to what is.

Q. What would you like to be written on your tombstone or how would you like to be remembered?

A. I don't really care if I am remembered. This body is going to be here and then it won't. People remembering it is not going to make any difference. All there is, is now. A lot of people try to get into the now. But I recommend that you try to get out of it. See if you can. You'll discover that you can't because the now is all there is. Life only happens now. As you discover this, things get easier. It also is just what is.

Q. Anything else?

A. I don't feel like I ever speak or do anything. This body is being used for a particular purpose. I'm just grateful it is being used this way. It's not something I can take personal credit for.

Hale on Letting Go, the movie

Q. Why did you make the movie *Letting Go*?

A. The movie actually created itself. We originally filmed the seminar that appears in the movie because we were going to create a DVD product of the event. Before the event was even over, I got this inner sense that it needed to be a movie, as opposed to a DVD of the seminar. Then the film just took on a life of its own.

Q. What is the main message of the film?

A. There are several messages. The first is to inspire people to love their fellow humans and the planet and then do something about it. The second is to help people evolve from human doings to human beings—and from human consumers to human caregivers for the earth. That's the overarching goal. On a more practical level, we want people to see that feelings are not who they are. Feelings are just feelings and you can let them go because you are already whole, perfect, and complete as you are. Not in some future time or place but right here, right now. We also want to give some practical tools so you can experience that on your own.

Q. In the film you say, "Be open to the possibility that [the feelings] will never come up again." Why did you say this about processing?

A. Any time you do this process, it's possible that you'll never need to do it again because it's done. I've seen that happen over and over, especially with the "triple welcoming" technique that's in the film. That technique evolved from two different things: one, it naturally evolved out of our seven-day retreat; two it came out of my participation in a world peace festival that never actually happened. For the festival, my wife and I discussed what I would say if I had just five or ten minutes to communicate to the planet. As far as techniques are concerned, I would communicate the triple welcoming one because it's just so powerful.

Q. In the film, you tell a man grieving the loss of his wife that he can keep the joy without the suffering. Why is this important to communicate?

A. People grieving have a misconception that they need to hold on to the grief; otherwise they will lose the person they love. It's not true. When you let go of the grief, the love you feel for the person deepens. That's because what you love about the person is still in your heart—and you may miss that if you just grieve. Of course, some grieving is appropriate. If you lose a loved one and you don't grieve, that's unnatural. But people often grieve way longer than they need to. When you're ready to let go, you'll find there is a deepening of the love. I've seen this in thousands of people as well as in my own life.

Hale on The Sedona Method, the book

Q. In the book *The Sedona Method*, you quote Lester Levenson as having said, "Bank in the bank, not in your head." What did he mean?

A. "Fake it until you make it" and "Tell the story the way you want it to be" are an I owe you (IOU) for trouble because so many people substitute fantasy for what's actually here. It's one of the biggest places I see people fall down when they are trying to create abundance, a better relationship, or health with the Law of Attraction and goals in general. If you are pretending, you start to believe your fantasy and it comes as a big shock when your body falls over sick, even though you've been seeing all the signs.

When you "fake it until you make it," what you're doing is something Lester used to call "head banking." Instead of banking in the bank, you're banking in your head. When you're banking in your head, your bank account gets empty. Of course there's nothing wrong with holding the positive in mind. But in my experience, there's something much more powerful. It's uncovering the positive that is already here right now. That requires no effort and doesn't cause distortion.

So I recommend you deal with what is and let go. The more you let go, the more you uncover the beauty that's already right here, right now. You uncover your intuitive knowingness, which is guiding you down exactly the right path in every moment. It's really that simple.

Q. Lester Levenson also said, "Even the impossible becomes completely possible when you are fully released on it." Can you tell us more?

A. The only limits we have are the ones we impose on ourselves. The biggest one is that we are separate from what is. You have never been separate. You are already the whole. You just forget because you are playing a role that you have started to identify with. When you see through that, things dramatically shift in a positive way. On a more practical level, when you let go you see that the limits aren't real. They have never been there. That makes a huge difference.

"When the world says, 'Give up,' Hope whispers, 'Try it one more time.'"

-Anonymous

"There are no accidents, only blessings in disguise."
Alicia Fall, Founder of Her Many Voices

Alicia Fall is a songwriter, lyricist, singer, and musician who draws upon her rich cultural background—Eastern Band Cherokee, Danish, Cuban, and Spanish—to capture the American experience. Alicia grew up in New York City, where she collaborated with jazz greats such as Chico Freeman and Norman Hedman. In 1998, she worked with musician Jon Solomon to release her premier CD, *Headed for Amsterdam*. The CD, a mix of jazz, blues, and soft rock, addresses the heartbreaking reality of human relationships. Her latest CD, *Hope Is What We Got*, was released in December 2008, with proceeds going to global causes. Alicia is a powerful performer who evokes spiritual awakening and emotional resonance from her audiences.

Q. What experiences put you on your spiritual path?
A. We come into the world on our spiritual path. It was my mother who nurtured and guided me on my journey. She is a deeply spiritual woman who taught me to be who I am, embrace my purpose, and recognize the connection among us all. Seeing the face of God in everything and everyone helps me appreciate life's blessings.

Q. How did these experiences change you?
A. I recognize the perfection in, and purpose behind, every moment. For example, my car was rear-ended and I sustained tears in my shoulders. When the doctors did an MRI, they found a bone tumor embedded in my left shoulder. Had this car crash not happened, I might have discovered this tumor too late. There are no accidents, only blessings in disguise. We experience these divine interventions all the time, but sometimes overlook them when they are not what we like or expect.

Q. What has been the most challenging part of your path?

A. Following my life purpose—my spiritual path—and making a living. For instance, sometimes I think I don't have all the resources needed to build Her Many Voices, my global awareness media production company focused on the positive transformation of women, children, and Mother Earth. But I have faith the resources will come. In fact they're already here, I just need to focus on them rather than the lack in my life. I'm not really lacking anything. I'm well cared for and stress only in moments. My friend and Lakota Sioux spiritual leader, Lee Plenty Wolf, summed it up as follows, "I'm walking somewhere between Spirit and survival."

Q. What changes are you noticing about your life and the world?

A. Since choosing my path, I am amazed by people's support. I'll meet someone and they'll say, "I don't know why, but I'm supposed to help you. I believe in what you're doing." I'll also hear songs on the radio or conversations in coffee shops that speak to me, and I'm reminded of Maya Angelou when she said, "I will step out on the word of God." I know that Spirit speaks to me all the time—to all of us. We just need to listen. When I trust, I receive all I need.

Q. What changes are others noticing about you?

A. People say I have more inner peace and conviction. I'm coming more from a place of focused faith, and not fear. I recently participated in a fundraiser to release the Sudanese slaves. I worked alongside Pastor Heidi McGinness, journalist Tamara Banks, and Dr. Annelle Norman, who hosted the event. My daughter came up afterwards and said, "Mom, I am so proud of you." There's nothing better than hearing this acknowledgement from your child and realizing others are sharing in your support.

Q. What is your earliest memory? Why do you remember it?

A. My earliest memories are of the openhearted women in my family. At age one-and-a half, I remember my mom tickling me in my crib. At age three, I remember bounding up the stairs and running into my grandmother's outstretched arms. These memories are gifts. They remind me of who I am and where I came from.

Q. Who are your mentors? What have you learned from them?
A. My mother who showed me how to love and walk my spiritual path. My sister, whose powerful self-expression as a dancer encouraged me to become a musician. We recently performed together for the first time at Lincoln Center. Jensine Larsen, founder of World Pulse Magazine, whose commitment to giving women and children a voice in the world has had an incredible ripple effect. My daughters, Melissa and Chenoa, who live their lives with such beauty. Melissa is a singer with an extraordinary voice and message. Chenoa practices karate and recently broke boards with her bare hands and feet. Afterwards, she exclaimed, "Mama, I'm so proud of myself. Now, I know I can do anything." I use her broken boards as inspiration to get me through difficult tasks. My daughter's partner, Lia, who has such drive and passion for helping people.

Q. What is the biggest challenge facing society?
A. The biggest challenge is recognizing we're all connected. It's not about blame—us versus them. It's about honoring our common bond and being responsible for each other. Fear gets in the way when people believe that if one group wins, another has to lose. The truth is that when I support you, you support me and all of society is lifted. When we understand this concept, there will be peace.

Q. What advice would you give someone just starting his or her spiritual path?
A. Listen without judgment, especially of yourself, because we often are our most harsh critics. Stop and fully embrace each moment, person, and/or thing. Spirit is speaking all the time if we would only listen.

Q. What are your practices for connecting to your higher purpose?
A. I spend time being quiet. I connect with people through meaningful conversation. I play music with others and by myself, blending eclectic styles such as Latin, jazz, blues, and soft rock. I appreciate art in all its forms.

Q. How do you use these practices when you get out of balance?
A. I take a deep breath and seek counsel from someone who can provide perspective. At night, I sometimes feel fear about getting my needs met and a committee of stressed voices will resound in my head. When this happens, I remind myself to trust God and the support people offer.

Q. How do you balance planning with remaining open to opportunity?
A. In the past, I lived with minimal planning, being open to guidance as it came. Now that I am leading Her Many Voices, I have a team that relies on me to set direction. So I asked to learn about planning and received support in the form of my colleague giving me a calendar. I saw my tasks listed there and smiled. Another divine intervention. I'm finally comfortable being an artist, spiritualist, and businesswoman.

Q. If you received $100,000, how would you spend it?
A. I would pay for the office space I just found for Her Many Voices. I would fund the salaries needed to attract qualified professionals to our social profit organization. I would pay off bills and donate the rest to World Pulse. I first heard about World Pulse when founder Jensine Larsen held the organization's first fundraiser in Portland, Oregon. Jensine so spoke to my soul that I volunteered to perform music at the event in front of sixty participants. The experience expanded my horizons, transitioning me from doing humanitarian work for the Native community to doing humanitarian work for the world.

Q. If you had thirty seconds with someone in an elevator, what three things would you tell the person to do to be joyful, peaceful, and whole?
A. Be still at some point each day. Look into the eyes of the person to whom you are speaking and recognize that he or she is your neighbor—the face of God. Accept and enjoy every moment—your happiness as well as your frustration. Stand tall and tell your story.

Q. What books or resources have helped you the most? Why?
A. *Conversations with God: An Uncommon Dialogue* (the Trilogy), by Neale Donald Walsch. I have read his books every day for ten years because they remind me to walk the path. I also draw strength, peace, and understanding from listening to people's stories and appreciating music and the arts.

Q. What would you like to be written on your tombstone?
A. I'm not planning to have a tombstone. Ideally, I would like to have my body left out so the animals can receive nourishment from my remains. Since we do not allow this practice anymore, I will have my ashes spread in a serene place. If I did have a tombstone, it would read, "It might not have been what she wanted, but she made her own choices." I say this because I'm responsible for my path. When things don't go my way, I don't say, "If only." I say, "Okay, I accept my choice," and continue on.

Q. Anything else?
A. When I was young, I stayed with different friends for six months while between apartments. One day I complained about bouncing from place to place to a friend who happened to be homeless. He replied, "Wow, you have a lot of friends!" This insight caused a permanent shift inside me. Life is all in how we look at it.

"For one human being to love another; that is perhaps the most difficult of all our tasks, the ultimate, the last test and proof, the work for which all other work is but preparation."

-Rainer Maria Rilke, *Letters to a Young Poet*

"Burn brightly. Hold nothing back."
Jamy Faust, Cofounder, Healing Arts of Belmont

Jamy has been practicing approaches to opening the mind, heart, and soul for most of her life. She has a master's degree in holistic counseling and psychology and is a graduate and former faculty member of the Barbara Brennan School of Healing. Jamy is extensively trained in Bert Hellinger's Family Constellation Work and Ralph Metzner's Alchemical Divination method. She blends energy healing, counseling, constellation facilitation, and guided imagery divination into her private practice with individuals and couples. Together with her husband Peter, Jamy has created The Constellation Approach—seminars and learning programs combining the modalities of family constellation work, energy medicine, and the awakening of consciousness.

Q. What experiences put you on your spiritual path?
A. I was eight years old when I recognized something much larger than me while singing in the church choir on Sunday. I felt a sense of wonderment, awe, and oneness with all that was around me—I'd had a sense of God. As a young woman, I moved to Hawaii to attend university when I learned my father had terminal cancer. I returned home to Boston and three days after my twentieth birthday, he died. His passing caused me to evaluate everything in my life and begin seeking spiritual answers.

Q. How did these experiences change you?
A. Not long after returning to Hawaii, I was waiting at the bus stop and met a woman from a Tibetan Buddhist meditation center. Our bus never came, so we ended up sharing our life stories over the course of three hours. She invited me to her meditation group and I went regularly. These experiences opened up my New England, Catholic world and I decided to

live in the Buddhist community for three years.

Q. What changes are you noticing about your life and the world?
A. When I allow myself, I am able to see the world through a broader lens that is not constrained by my emotions. This isn't automatic, but if I slow down enough, my perception opens. I try to own my issues and be authentic in relationships. I can be very attuned to the needs of others and now I'm becoming more aware of a larger connection to all that is, from the microcosm of the family to the macrocosm of the world and universe. We swim in a much larger stream of consciousness and are influenced by everything in the cosmos.

Q. What changes are others noticing about you?
A. I think my husband and friends accept who I've become but it seems to have taken my family longer. As the oldest of seven, I held an idea of who I was supposed to be, rather than just being myself with them. A few years ago, my mother had a terrible cold that wouldn't go away. I asked her to come in for a healing. She did and her cold was better in a day. She appreciated what I did so much that she told everyone in the family. At first I thought she said nice things because she was my mother. Then I realized she sincerely meant her compliments. She and my other family members now really appreciate me and the work I do in the world.

Q. What has been the most challenging part of your path?
A. I learn from extremes. Coming from a big family, and then moving alone to Hawaii. Living a quiet, spiritual life in the Buddhist meditation center, then entering the fast paced, glamorous world of Hawaiian hotels and tourism. I was never sure how to integrate these two sides of the pendulum—the introverted spiritual seeker and the extroverted life experiencer. I wanted to balance them as well as cultivate a relationship with my new husband, Peter. When we moved to a private Caribbean island to manage a resort, we had more

time to mediate and develop our spirituality as a couple. We also met world renowned energy healer, Barbara Brennan, who was vacationing on the island with her husband. She invited us to experience her healing program and we chose to enroll in her four-year school.

Now, after twenty-three years of marriage and living, working, and teaching together, I realize my greatest spiritual challenge is my relationship with my husband. Marriage has been one of the toughest—and most rewarding—spiritual paths. I am so grateful to be able to share my journey with him.

Q. What is your earliest memory? Why do you remember it?
A. I remember being in a bassinette and looking at the room around me, especially the beautiful patterns on the walls. I must have been between two and six months of age. These were the walls of my maternal grandparents' living room. I loved my grandparents very much and I remember the walls because they help me feel connected to my grandmother and grandfather.

Q. Who are your mentors? What have you learned from them?
A. Prior to becoming a healer, I had many informal mentors. The first was practice of Catholicism with its rituals, beauty, and rigorous education. The nuns who taught me were kind and encouraged my learning. One Dominican nun, Sister Mary Laura, was probably the happiest person I've ever met. As a preteen, I found a sweet and long-lasting male friend, who introduced me to the Christian philosopher, Pierre Teilhard de Chardin and a word called "consciousness." In Hawaii, my college outrigger canoe coach mentored me to become part of the first eighteen-woman crew to cross the forty-two-mile Molokai Channel. After college, the writings of Tibetan Buddhist leader Chögyam Trungpa Rinpoche taught me how to integrate beingness into my life. And due to his influence, I was initiated into the Kagyu lineage by the sixteenth Kar-

mapa, Rangjung Rigpei Dorje. In fact, the ten years I lived in Hawaii helped me experience nature, my body, and soul more completely. Two other mentors were music, which continues to enliven my soul, and Jane Robert's book, The Seth Material, which opened me to the concept of mediums and channeling.

When I began studying healing, I sought out formal mentors such as:
• Karin Aarons, who continues to remind me to be present and is my greatest mentor and friend.

• Barbara Brennan, who taught me how to work with the personal (or human) energy field in her school of healing.

• Bert Hellinger, who trained me to work with the family soul using the Family Constellation Method, a method for releasing entanglements within our families and relationships so we can experience life more fully.

• Ralph Metzner, who helped me expand into the collective soul and the cosmology of consciousness using Alchemical Divination, a process for healing the past and accessing guidance and vision for the future.

I blend these concepts in my healing practice to create an organic, holistic approach that expands a person's health, well-being, and consciousness.

Q. What is the greatest challenge facing society?
A. People thinking they are right. Rightness makes it difficult to see other viewpoints, which can cause conflict and war. I encourage individuals to step into other people's shoes and see the world through their eyes. This experience shifts them out of needing to be right to recognizing we are all one.

Q. What advice would you give someone just starting his or her spiritual path?

A. When you start a spiritual path, don't swallow it whole. Incorporate the parts that make sense and leave the rest. Spending time in nature or meditation helps you make this discernment. You hold your own energy and find what you need rather than lose yourself to the path.

Q. What are your spiritual practices for connecting to your higher purpose?

A. Yoga! And I love making beautiful spaces, especially in my home. It's like meditation to play with color in fabrics and flowers to create things like altars. I also work on cherishing and cultivating deep love for my husband. That's been my greatest spiritual practice to connect me with my higher purpose. We have chosen to be together and I treasure the experience of sharing our lives fully.

Q. How do you use these practices when you get out of balance?

A. When I get out of balance, I stop what I'm doing, recognize what's happening, and shift in the moment. If I cannot shift right away, I wait patiently until I do. After many years of practice, my recovery time has become much shorter. Sometimes I get frustrated and think, *I already worked on this fear, so why am I here again?* Then I remember it's just a way to reconnect with my power and continue growing.

Q. How do you balance planning with remaining open to opportunity?

A. I feel that I'm comfortable being a risk taker and lean easily into opportunity. The plans can be reworked later.

Q. If you received $100,000, how would you spend it?

A. I would give some to family members who are hurting financially. I would use the rest to create a beautiful healing center, or urban temple, where people could come to rejuvenate through meditation and prayer. The building next door is available, so when you send the check, I will build it. I'm teasing!

Q. If you had thirty seconds with someone in an elevator, what three things would you tell the person to do to be joyful, peaceful, and whole?
A. Don't worry about being right. Instead, let yourself see the world through another person's eyes. Recognize that your life is perfect the way it is; there is nothing wrong. Take time to rest.

Q. What books or resources have helped you the most? Why?
A. I recommend *The Second Half of Life: Opening the Eight Gates of Wisdom*, by Angeles Arrien. The guidance she offers is helpful to people in midlife. I also like poetry such as Rainer Maria Rilke's poems in *The Book of Hours*, translated by Anita Barrows and Joanna Macy and *The Gift*, by Hafiz. Poetry takes us out of our daily routine into a more expansive mind. For example, Rilke writes, ". . . You, sent out beyond your recall, go to the limits of your longing. Embody me. / Flare up like flame and make big shadows I can move in. / Let everything happen to you: beauty and terror. Just keep going. No feeling is final . . ."

I live life with an open heart, burning brightly and holding nothing back. When my life is over, I will smolder into ashes.

Q. What would you like to be written on your tombstone?
A. I won't have a tombstone. After I am cremated, I would like my ashes thrown off a cliff into the ocean just north of Kailua Kona, Hawaii. I hope people will say that it was my agreement to live a path with heart and that I did so.

Q. Anything else?
A. Each time I work with new teachings, I understand better what my other teachers were saying. For example, Metzner put into language Hellinger's unwritten concepts and Hellinger

sealed my understanding of the energy field Brennan envisioned. In recent meditations, I've seen the soul agreements I made for this life and recall being at a council of souls, seeing my parents' energy and agreeing to be their daughter, and they, in turn, agreeing to be my parents. This is one small illustration of the consciousness expansion that is moving me now. As I expand, I begin to accept everything, realizing I have agreed to it all. This acceptance gives me great peace as I let go of struggle and open my heart wide.

"Why should I wish to see God better than this day?
I see something of God each hour of the twenty-four, and each moment then;
In the faces of men and women I see God, and in my own face in the glass."

-Walt Whitman, *Leaves of Grass*

"People are trying to find God without all the religion."
Hugh Halter, Community Missionary and Author of *The Tangible Kingdom*

Hugh Halter is the national director of Missio, a global network of missional leaders and church planters. He also is a specialist with Church Resource Ministries and the lead architect of Adullam, a congregational network of incarnational communities. Hugh has authored two books, *The Tangible Kingdom* and *The Sacrilegious Disciple*. He currently lives in Denver with his wife Cheryl and his children, Ryan, Alli, and Mckenna.

Q. What experiences put you on your spiritual path?
A. I grew up in a conservative Christian family that faced many challenges: my sister's mental illness, my dad's unemployment, and my parents' eventual divorce. During this time, I questioned God's existence. The idea that God was up there and we are down here never made sense to me. Neither did going to church. Having a personal relationship with Jesus helped me survive and hold my family together.

Q. How did these experiences change you?
A. My family's struggles led me to my spiritual calling early in life. In college I majored in psychology and religion and become involved in campus ministry due to my compassion for people with mental illness and the suicides of some friends. I found mentors in the ministry and people started to follow me. I came to ministry from my personal relationship with Christ, not from the church.

Q. What changes are you noticing about your life and the world?
A. Jesus said, "Whoever wishes to become great among you

shall be your servant, and whoever wishes to be first among you shall be your slave." (Matthew 20:26-27) I did not become a spiritual leader by being the pastor of a church. I gained authority through modeling Christ's presence and an alternative way of life. As I adopted this posture, people began following me. Now I train church leaders worldwide, encouraging them to lead by being out in front, not on top.

Q. What changes are others noticing about you?
A. My wife says, "If Hugh did not start churches, he would probably never go to one." I am a community advocate whose mission is to embody God's kingdom on earth. I teach by pastoring to people's needs, not by elevating myself as a preacher. When people introduce me to others, they make this distinction by saying, "He's a pastor but he's not what you'd expect." Even my daughter says, "He's a pastor and he rides a Harley."

Q. What has been the most challenging part of your path?
A. Turning relationship ministry into organized church. I feel more comfortable being a neighborhood advocate than a church pastor. However, I recognize that people drift apart if they are not held together in a faith community. Sometimes I feel frustrated with people—including pastors—who want to attend church but not engage in the world. I teach them to act like missionaries, to embody the faith on the street and see what God does. The most powerful spiritual things happen through spontaneous interruption.

Q. What is your earliest memory? Why do you remember it?
A. At age six my friend Jimmy and I were playing in the sandbox with a Batman car that shot rockets. This was the first of many happy childhood memories. Despite their rocky relationship, my parents always loved and cared for us.

Q. Who are your mentors? What have you learned from them?
A. Leland, my Sunday school teacher, who was the first Christian

guy I really liked. Dave, who got me into organized ministry through Youth for Christ. Steve Ridgway, my mentor in college, who introduced me to spiritual leadership and missionary work. Through serving the community, Steve inspired hundreds of people to follow Christ.

Q. What is the greatest challenge facing society?
A. Creating religious community so we embody God rather than suffocate him. Our failings cause us to create institutions that paint an ugly picture of God. For example, a third of Catholic school children in Ireland were molested during the 1970s. This atrocity is why people seek God outside of religion. It's also why people embraced Jesus. He spoke about a new kingdom, free of religious and political oppression, in which we unite in our love for God and one another. Jesus' incarnation took the abstract concept of God and made it relevant to people's daily lives. The early Christians understood this and spread his message of mercy and compassion to change the world.

Q. What advice would you give someone just starting his or her spiritual path?
A. Our society is too self-absorbed. People say they're trying to find themselves, but they're really trying to lose themselves. Free yourself from this pain by giving to others. When you give, you feel good because you are connected to all of life. Right now, go out and do something to help someone.

Q. What are your spiritual practices for connecting to your higher purpose?
A. I experience God most when I am physically active and/or serving others. For example, I get up early and talk to God while walking around the lake. I ask, "Is there anything you want to tell me?" and God replies in a flood of thoughts. I also hear him when I ride my Harley, go fly-fishing with friends, or talk to people in the neighborhood. I feel least close to God when giving a sermon. It's a duty I perform to

help others connect.

Q. How do you use these practices when you get out of balance?
A. I usually feel down after leading organized church gatherings. To gain perspective, I call friends and fellow pastors who understand what I'm going through and support me. I also exercise and sit in the sauna to clear out and start moving again.

Q. How do you balance planning with remaining open to opportunity?
A. On Sunday evenings I light a candle, pour a glass of wine, and plan out my week. I schedule time to be with my family, faith community, and church leaders-in-training while leaving plenty of room to be available to God and my neighbors. For example, I write my sermons in the coffee shop and work out with friends and acquaintances. If I didn't make this time, I would get buried in a church office where God couldn't interrupt me even if he wanted to! In our spiritual formation class, we teach Christians to get out and be with others so God can do his work.

Q. If you received $100,000, how would you spend it?
A. I'd support young spiritual leaders with a passion for community missionary work. I'd help loved ones get out of debt. I'd take my wife on a nice vacation because she has given up a lot for ministry life. I'd do something to bless my family.

Q. If you had thirty seconds with someone in an elevator, what three things would you tell the person to do to be joyful, peaceful, and whole?
A. I'm an evangelist, but I don't start a conversation about God unless I can develop a relationship with the person. God's kingdom is so immense that I would do it an injustice to boil it down into a few pithy phrases. If Jesus spent his life as a carpenter and became the savior of the world, I can relax and just be with people.

Q. What books or resources have helped you the most? Why?
A. Community missionaries who make God's kingdom tangible to people outside the church inspire me. I personally am motivated to live this way and am finding more and more spiritual leaders who are. We don't want to just lead a church, we want to be God's heart in the world. My book, *The Tangible Kingdom*, discusses this desire in a very personal way.

Q. What would you like to be written on your tombstone?
A. "Hugh Halter, an inspiring peasant. He was an ordinary guy who lived an extraordinary experience."

Q. Anything else?
A. I am writing another book called *The Sacrilegious Disciple*, which is about being an antireligious God follower. In the past, I hated writing. But my book agent said, "Write like you talk and say what's in your heart," so that's what I did and he cleaned it up into a book. I keep writing because people are seeking God without all the religion. I want to be there to support them. People will never stop seeking because "God has set eternity in their heart." (Ecclesiastes 3:11)

"First keep the peace within yourself, then you can also bring peace to others."

-Thomas A. Kempis

""What's the meaning of life? To celebrate our magnificence!"
Hank Innerfeld, Spiritual Healer, Speaker, Teacher, and Author

Hank Innerfeld is a healing practitioner, motivational speaker, spiritual teacher, and author trained in a number of healing modalities. He has published two books, *Messages to Your Heart* and *Soul Messages*, and gives presentations and classes throughout the U.S. Hank has successfully treated thousands of clients around the world using Spiritual Response Therapy (SRT), Spiritual Restructuring (SpR), and other techniques to empower their lives. Hank is an ordained minister who is certified by the Spiritual Response Association to teach these forms of spiritual healing. He currently lives in Colorado with his partner Dawn.

Q. What experiences put you on your spiritual path?
A. I've always wanted to know why things work the way they do. This led me to ask lots of questions and later become a scientist and engineer. Then, fifteen years ago, I was dragged kicking and screaming into the healing arena. At first I was not a willing camper because I wanted to do things my way. For example, in a martial arts class, I went down six times (on a hardwood floor) before I finally accepted that a technique would drop me like a sack of potatoes. So it was an evolutionary process in which I eventually learned to listen to my inner guidance and get out of my own way. Since doing that, life has become a marvelous adventure. Every experience, no matter how joyful or painful, is magnificent. We create these experiences for our growth so we might as well enjoy them.

I have written two books. The first, *Messages to Your Heart: Insights and Understanding to Empower Your Life*, helps people get in touch with their heart felt guidance so they can make conscious, proactive choices. The second, *Soul Messages: Insights and Understandings to Expand into Life*, paints a picture of life from the soul's perspective. Religion teaches that we have a soul, but we don't know much beyond that. It's like how people see the glass as half full or half empty—but they forget that there's a glass! Once you see the glass, you realize there's a whole universe beyond it. Then it doesn't matter if your glass is half full or half empty. What matters is recognizing that your choices, whether joyful or painful, are all positive because they help you grow. From that perspective, you start to understand the universal laws governing our lives and the bigger picture comes into focus.

Q. How did these experiences change you?
A. As we become aware of these universal laws, we see that reality is governed by our beliefs and perceptions, what some traditions call our thoughts, words, and deeds. When we change these, our life experience changes. This is ironic because we can be so dogmatic about the way life is. But in truth, that's just our belief about the way life is. So regardless of whether we believe something is true or isn't, we're right. Whatever we believe will evolve and become our reality.

With this awareness, I flow in inner peace, unconditional love, total acceptance, and allowance of everything that happens. I honor people's choices without getting caught up in drama because I know it's their own creation for their growth. I see the perfection in every situation and can listen to my inner guidance to make a positive impact. This gives me a perspective that is fundamentally different from most people. But it affords an inner peace and love that many don't have. It's like the ancient Sanskrit word namaste, which is used in India as a greeting. It means, "I honor the place in you in which the entire universe dwells . . . which is of love, integrity, wisdom, and peace. When you are in that place in you and I am in that place in me, we are one." When I live in this way, there is ease, peace, and joy. Most people in the Western world don't even know this way of life is a possibility.

Q. What has been the most challenging part of your path?
A. Getting out of my own way. When I was a scientist and engineer, everything had to be my way. Now when I do those crazy antics, I laugh at myself. I realize how ridiculous they are in terms of the larger picture. The second biggest challenge was loving myself fully and completely. I spent so much time focusing on the past and future that I didn't recognize the perfection of each moment. And this moment is the only thing I really have control over. We're so caught up in our thoughts and to-dos that we don't spend time just being. We've become human doings rather than human beings. Ironically, our real work is all about being fully present in the moment, listening to our inner guidance, and unconditionally accepting and loving others and ourselves. This allows us to recognize that every experience is perfect for our growth. So we can flow into moments rather than resist them. Sometimes we dig in our heels and recreate yesterday's pain instead of risking something new that could improve it. We do this even though we know the only constant from birth to death is change.

Q. What changes are you noticing about your life and the world?
A. My choices create my experience, just as your choices create your experience. I can't change you and you can't change me. So the only person I have control over is me. And as I change myself, people can notice and say, "I can do that too." Again, it is important to remember every choice we make is perfect for our growth. Some choices result in painful experiences, others in joyful ones, but they all help us grow. The choices I make help me be a sea of calm amidst an ocean of chaos. They help me contribute to humankind's awakening

by holding a frequency of unconditional love and peace. It's not that I do this consciously. It's just a result of the choices I make. When a critical mass of us does this, we will awaken humanity. It's going to happen. It's just a matter of when—and that depends on each of us. Again, I can't choose for you, but I have made the commitment to hold that tone for myself, to be that sea of calm that will help create an ocean of peace.

I'm sure a lot of people you've interviewed say similar things because it's what's happening right now. The Earth's population is swelling because we have souls stampeding to experience humankind's graduation from in-body. Ninety-nine percent of the world's population is going to get there and not have a clue how they did. Those of us with some understanding can provide them with awareness. We can say we are evolving from mind-felt consciousness to heartfelt consciousness. Mind-felt consciousness was about being controlled by fear, scarcity, power, limitation, control, and survival of the fittest. Heartfelt consciousness is about love, abundance, acceptance, allowance, inner peace, and community. We are between the two consciousness paradigms right now. In fact, we are in the birth canal going through spasms. Many women who have had children say childbirth was one of the greatest experiences of their lives. But if you ask them about this experience when they're having contractions every few seconds, you're going to get a very different answer. It's the same way with our evolution.

The world seems chaotic right now but it's really a perfect orchestration to get us to the point where we are so challenged that we will be forced to try something new. Unfortunately, thanks to the media, people have become so fearful of this orchestration that they are not staying in their power. They are just drifting through life. When things really come to a head, people will start banding together to do things differently, which will help build this new community and societal paradigm. The U.S. will have a major role to play in humankind's awakening.

Q. What changes are others noticing about you?
A. You would have to ask them. My family members—aside from my former partner, brother, and children—have little to do with me. They think I am way too "out there." But I have good relationships with people in my extended circle. For example, I was talking to this guy after a presentation and I got the sense that he really liked me and wanted to be my friend. It surprised me because it was just a casual chat. I told my partner Dawn and she said, "You don't realize the impact you have on people. You don't know how loved you are." She's right, I don't. But I do feel incredibly loved.

Q. What is your earliest memory? Why do you remember it?
A. When I was twelve years old, we went to visit my grandmother at the nursing home. We parked our car on a hill and my parents got out. I was in the backseat holding shopping bags that were part of her weekly care package. My father forgot to put the emergency brake on and the car started rolling down the hill. My mother screamed as my father tried to hold it. The next thing I knew, I was in the driver's seat with my foot on the brake. At that age, I didn't even know what the brake was, but somehow I managed to stop the car. I had forgotten this happened until my mother reminded me years later saying she'd never seen anybody move so fast. In that state of emergency, I unknowingly drew upon universal laws like bilocation—the ability to be in two places—to prevent the accident. For the past twenty-five years, I have been trying to bilocate again, but haven't been successful.

Aside from that, I don't remember much about my childhood. I do remember my inner sense of feeling, clairsentience, being acutely developed at an early age. I get a feeling, then a knowing, and it's incredible how accurate it is. I use this inner sense with my clients to get right to their core issues. For example, this morning I had a business meeting with a guy who has some chest problems. In the course of our discussion, I shared some things with him and by the time he left, his heart relaxed and he was breathing more deeply. Even though it wasn't a healing session, I was still able to help him. Actually, I had to learn how to filter my clairsentience so I don't take too much in. Like the first time I worked with somebody with hemorrhoids and was squirming for hours afterwards!

I'm a master dowser and use it every day to figure out what's contributing to my clients' symptoms and how to best treat them. Scientists have done brain scans on spiritual practitioners like dowsers, healers, yogis, and so forth. What they've found is that these groups have more brain wave activity than the average person. They use all the frequencies—alpha, beta, theta, delta, and gamma—whereas most people use primarily beta. So I'm just using more brain frequencies, which allows insights to come through. But everybody can do this. I have had people in my dowsing classes as young as nine and as old as eighty.

Q. Who are your mentors? What have you learned from them?
A. I have never had long-term teachers, but people have always come into my life to help me on my path. One person I really admire is the Dalai Lama. He came to New Jersey when I was living there but the tickets were $250-$1,000. My family didn't have the means to do that so I put it out there that I wanted to see him through an affordable venue. The next night, I went to tai chi class where a visitor told us that everyone on the mailing list of a Tibetan Buddhist monastery in Washington, New Jersey would receive two tickets to see the Dalai Lama. So of course, the next day I was on the mailing list.

My former partner, our daughter and her boyfriend, and two friends and I all piled into a van and drove out to the monastery amidst torrential rain. We got there around noon and the Dalai Lama wasn't going to speak until 2:30 p.m., so we toured the grounds and then sat down on our blanket to meditate. The rain stopped and we were in the second row of the field behind the area reserved for Tibetan nationals. During my meditation, I was gushing with gratitude to the Dalai Lama for honoring us with his presence. The message I got back was, *No, it is not I who needs to be honored. It is all of you.* At first I was embarrassed to share this with my daughter and her boyfriend, but it turned out they had gotten a similar message. It gets me choked up just thinking about it. The Dalai Lama honored us for finding time for spirituality in our busy, secular lives.

By the time His Holiness came out to speak, there were 8,000 people in the field. When he stood on the balcony, you could feel a wave of love ripple across the crowd. Three butterflies landed on the railing in front of him and didn't move until he finished talking an hour and a half later. There were also hawks circling overhead. He was speaking in guttural Tibetan with a translator. It was a very powerful experience. Just remembering it makes my heart sing.

So that was a pivotal point in my life, as was the Harmonic Convergence in August 1987 and the 11:11 activities in January 199Q. I guess I have been applying my energies towards the awakening of humanity for some time now, even though I wasn't consciously aware of it.

Q. What is the biggest challenge facing society?
A. Change. We resist change like crazy, especially in these tough economic times. It's like that saying, "If you always do what you've always done, you'll always get what you've always got." Many people are doing things that never worked before but only fifteen times harder—and they're expecting different results. I think that's what Einstein called insanity and what I call resisting change. We are at a point in our evolu-

tion where if we don't change, things are going to get harder until we are forced to. When we look at the bigger picture, we realize that we're creating this entire scenario and it's a perfection orchestration. For example, former President Bush's sending troops to Iraq led to fifteen million people around the world uniting to protest for peace. You know how the Bible says, "For where two or three have gathered in my name, I am there?" (Matthew 18:20) Unbeknownst to Bush, his action will usher in a lasting peace the likes of which we have never seen. So it's just a matter of where we choose to focus our thoughts and energies.

Q. What advice would you give someone just starting his or her spiritual path?
A. First, learn to listen to your inner guidance. It will always serve you. Second, recognize you are a magnificent being of God who is here to rediscover your divinity and create the life of your dreams. Third, know you are never alone. Separation is only an illusion. Finally, love yourself fully and unconditionally for the magnificence that you reflect to the world.

Q. What are your practices for connecting to your higher purpose?
A. I have been meditating for over twenty years. Now I'm at the point where I can just take a deep breath, connect to my higher consciousness, and flow with what comes. For example, on Valentine's Day, my daughter and I took a hike. On the mountaintop she said, "You've got a message. What is it?" I took a deep breath and out it came.

We're at a pivotal moment in history. The energetic spectrum bathing the planet is higher than it's been in the last 26,000 years. This spectrum is infusing us with incredible frequencies of light, causing the veil between the dimensions to thin. Love is a high frequency and fear, or the absence of love, is a low one. We must choose which to flow in—love or fear—because we can't be in both, just like a woman can't be almost pregnant. As these frequencies go even higher, it will become easier and easier to connect with our inner guidance. Every equinox, solstice, or similar event raises our vibration by opening the Earth's structure and allowing it to reflect back, and resonate with, the higher frequencies surrounding us.

So as these energies continue to go up, anything that's not from the light—anger, hatred, fear—will surface to be dealt with. If we choose to remain stuck, then this discord will come right back in our face the next time there's a frequency shift. You see, our growth moves in an upward spiral. If we were to look at the spiral from the top two-dimensionally, it would look like a circle. If we were revisiting an old trauma represented by a point on the circle, it might look like we were revisiting the same spot over and over again. But when we look at the spiral three-dimensionally, we see that the trauma is at a much higher point on the spiral. And what we're really dealing with is only the residue of the old trauma anchored at a higher frequency. So instead of saying, "Oh my God, I thought I dealt with this years ago," we can say, "Great! I am releasing the last remnants of this at a much higher vibration."

Q. How do you use these practices when you get out of balance?

A. I don't get caught up in things too frequently. But when I do, as soon as I become aware of it, I use the tools I teach in my classes to turn it around. It only takes a couple of seconds because I know it's not about anything outside of me, it's about something within me that needs to be released—and is perfect for my growth.

For example, last summer we moved into a new house. I was so busy that I barely had time to pack. As I rushed out with my first box, I broke my ankle on the curb. My first thought was, *Why did I do this?* Of course, it was to help me slow down. But I didn't at first. I kept teaching, seeing clients, and packing—all the while hobbling on crutches and wearing a cast.

A week later, I said to myself, *You should really slow down. That's why you broke your ankle in the first place!* So I started to do things more prudently, like thinking about what I could bring each time I went upstairs so I could minimize the number of trips. I've gotten to a certain age where I don't react so much anymore. Instead, I embrace each moment fully. This enables me to get more understanding and awareness. Then, each experience, even breaking my ankle, becomes a joy and an adventure.

I may have learned this from something that started off as a joke. When my teachers used to ask, "Are there any questions?" I would always play the smart ass and say, "Yeah, what's the meaning of life?" So one day when I was teaching Spiritual Response Therapy, I said, "Are there any questions? And, 'What is the meaning of life?' doesn't qualify as a question." Everybody chuckled. Then somebody said, "Yeah, what is the meaning of life?" Three or four others chimed in and said, "Yeah, that's a good question. What is it?" So I went into my inner guidance and asked. What I heard is that we are here to learn about and celebrate our own magnificence. So from a gag came one of my greatest learning experiences.

Q. How do you balance planning with remaining open to opportunity?
A. I don't think you want to use me as a role model. My partner Dawn is always saying, "Will you get focused on that?" When I was a scientist and engineer, I liked to plan and tack things down. Now that I've gotten out of my way, I flow into moments. I do have a general idea of what I want to accomplish. But when I am on the phone with a client, I don't worry about spending extra time. I know that's what needs to happen.

I do make lists of what I need to bring to my workshops. But when it comes time to speak, I simply clear myself and let the words come. Often I don't even remember what I've said. When I play back the audiotape I think, *That's pretty impressive. I never would have thought to put those two things together.* I spend more time in my right brain than my left. But since I was originally trained as a scientist and engineer, I am comfortable doing linear planning when needed.

By the way, even though our watches still show twenty-four hours in a day, time is no longer linear. The higher frequencies infusing our planet have sped up everything so we go through twenty-four hours now in only about twelve. This is one of the reasons people feel so stressed for time.

Q. If you received $100,000, how would you spend it?
A. Money is not really an issue for me. So I don't think about it too much. I focus more on people. But since you're asking, the first thing I'd do is invest it to quadruple the amount. Then I'd use some of it to help a person start a business. I'd give it to someone who is sincere about changing his or her life. This is because many people pay lip service to changing their financial situation but don't really mean it. I can't tell you how many spiritual people I know who say, "Okay God, I am here. Use me." But then they just sit on their hands. God feeds every bird but he doesn't put food in the nest. We have to go out and do something. These folks have actually created these challenges for themselves in order to transcend them. If I gave them money, I would be detracting from their growth.

Q. If you had thirty seconds with someone in an elevator, what three things would you tell the person to do to be joyful, peaceful, and whole?
A. Recognize that you are magnificent and perfect as you are. You always have been and you always will be. Saying this would help them reclaim their power and flow into a whole

new energy. Actually, now that I think about it, I'd have to find out more about the person. We're all at different parts of our growth path so what I'd say would depend on that. Because while it's true we are all perfect, what would best help the person is a message that would flow in the moment. For example, Tuula, has anybody told you that they love you today? [I say, "No."] Well, let me be the first. Tuula, I love you. You are special and you can have anything you choose in life. Notice how hard that was for you to receive. [I say, "Yes, it was."] So self-love is one of your core issues. I might say that to you in the elevator. When I do say that to people, I find that most can't receive it.

I have these types of thirty-second commercials with people every day, like the businessman who was here this morning. I encouraged him to make a couple of statements that opened his heart. His life is going to be different now because of the power of the word. After he made these statements, he gave a heartfelt belly laugh. His partner was shocked. He hasn't done that it years. Sometimes you can say just the right couple of words that will forever change someone. People call me all the time saying, "Oh my God, you changed my life." And I'll turn to my partner Dawn and say, "I don't have a clue what I said to them!"

This question really boils down to what life is all about. It's about how we touch others. There was a line in the movie *Ghost* that said, "The love inside, [it's the only thing] you take . . . with you." That's true. And it's the only thing that when we give it away, we get more of it in return.

Q. What books or resources have helped you the most? Why?
A. Everyone's spiritual path is different. Whatever the resources—music, nature, meditation—they all boil down to one thing: quieting the mind. When we quiet the mind, we have an easier time listening to our inner guidance and remembering our truth. In my book *Soul Messages*, I talk about

souls coming into bodies with the grandest of intentions to create heaven on Earth. Then they are bombarded with so many distractions that it gets like the saying, "When you are up to your neck in alligators, it's hard to remember that you came to drain the swamp."

So, in general, I would encourage people to quiet their minds using whatever resources work. I would also tell them to actively seek, rather than wait for it to come. And I would advise them to be open to possibilities beyond what they expect. For example, I've recently been thrown into situations where I've had to wing it at the last minute. The first was giving a presentation entitled Expand Your People Skills, Empower Your Relationships to the Optimist Club. When I arrived, I saw that everybody was retirement age and above. With that level of experience, I realized I needed to approach the topic from a different angle. So I started by telling a joke about a priest. In the joke, the priest is looking out a second-story window as floodwaters are rising. A man in a rowboat comes by and says, "Father, hop in and I'll take you to safety. The priest replies, "No my son. The Lord will save me. Save someone else." So the guy rows off. As the floodwaters continue to rise, two more people come and try to save him, one in a motorboat and the other in a helicopter. Each time, the priest refuses saying, "God will save me. Save somebody else." Eventually, the floodwaters overtake the priest and he drowns. When he gets to heaven, he angrily says, "God, I believed in you. I dedicated my life to you. How could you let me drown?" God replies, "What do you want from me? I sent you a rowboat, a motorboat, and a helicopter!"

This segue helped the audience open up to my sharing a different perspective on life, one that focuses on staying present in the moment so we can have fuller, richer interactions in our personal and professional lives. Incidentally, later that evening, I had another engagement in which I was supposed to give the last third of a talk. The other two speakers didn't show up so I ended up giving the whole presentation. It turned out really well because I followed my own advice and just stayed in the moment, connecting to my inner guidance and the audience.

The second time I had to wing it was during my first radio interview. Twelve seconds before we went on the air, the hostess' phone system went down. I said to the station manager, "Where did she go?" He replied, "She'll call in later. Okay, three, two, one, you are on the air." When we went on the air, I just started talking and it was a great experience. The show was later featured as the best of the week and the station manager told me that he was blown away. In one hour, I'd shared everything he'd learned in the past thirty years. So life is an adventure. Even though we are cocreating it, it might not always be in our comfort zone.

Q. What would you like to be written on your tombstone?
A. "A man who lived through his heart and profoundly touched others. A man who did his part to awaken humanity." As far as my body, I'll be cremated. No sense messing up the Earth.

But it's not about the legacy I leave behind. It's about how I touch people now. I live in each moment and do the best I can. That's not to say I can't improve. But as long as I do my best, then I know I'm making a difference. I recently had two people name their children after me. It was a hard thing to graciously accept. But I knew they had done this because I had touched their lives profoundly, and that touched my heart.

Q. Anything else?
A. There are a trillion snowflakes, but no two are alike. Embrace your uniqueness rather than trying to be like another snowflake. You are perfect as you are. You have incredible gifts and a unique part to play in humanity's awakening. So celebrate your magnificence and honor the divinity within

yourself and others. When you embrace life fully, every moment becomes joyful. There are no mistakes, only creations we have made for our growth.

I was at a birthday party a few summers ago where we had fourteen people seated around this big table. The restaurant was so noisy that I could only talk to the people on either side of me. The woman next to me had shoulder pain. So I took out my pendulum and start dowsing. Her pain went away and this guy a few seats away yelled, "What did you do?" I said, "I was dowsing to get rid of the pain in her shoulder." He was intrigued. Later, we were talking about gold prospecting and I passed around some gold nuggets and a small bar of silver I always carry with me. The guy said, "You lead such a fascinating life!" I said, "You can join me in any of these activities—gold prospecting, dowsing, and so on."

Most people sit back and wait for life to happen. I say, "Go out and embrace it. If you don't like what you're experiencing, create something new." Many people repeat the same painful situation over and over again when they don't have to. Learn from it and move on. Or, if you do repeat it, don't beat yourself up. Just say, "Oh, I did that again. I won't in the future." Celebrate your learning and keep going. *Namaste!*

"You will find as you look back upon your life that the moments when you have really lived are the moments when you have done things in the spirit of love."

-Henry Drummond

"Beyond all appearance, God is present."
Reverend Cynthia James, Mile Hi Church

Reverend Cynthia James is a lecturer, teacher, and author of the book What Will Set You Free. She is an internationally known performing artist and former talk show co-host in Los Angeles. She has counseled thousands of people and has facilitated hundreds of workshops and seminars that integrate traditional therapeutic techniques, music, creativity, and spiritual processes. She has been a featured speaker in business and spiritual forums. Cynthia graduated from two master's degree programs, one in spiritual psychology and one in consciousness studies. She currently serves as an associate minister at Mile Hi Church, one of the largest new thought spiritual centers in the world, with a congregation of over 10,000 people. She and her husband, Carl Studna, a world renowned photographer, live in the mountains of Colorado.

Q. What experiences put you on your spiritual path?
A. I have always been on a spiritual path. I grew up in the African Methodist Episcopal church and was surrounded by women in my family who were prophetic dreamers. Being intuitive was the norm in our family. As I stepped out into the world, I realized not everyone had these kinds of visions and dreams. When I became a singer and actress in my twenties, I realized I needed something to balance out the Hollywood syndrome I was in. Relationships were also a challenge because I was working out stuff from my violent and chaotic childhood. I found myself guided to a small religious science community in Los Angeles. Michael Beckwith was a Religious Science Practitioner and teacher there. I started taking classes with him and saw that my experiences as a performer were dovetailing with my work as a practitioner counseling people. I enrolled in a master's program in spiritual psychology and

began to understand that there was no separation, that if I knew who I was at the core, then my only job would be to show up and serve as a conduit for spirit. I could be a conduit whether I was in ministry, corporate America, or performing on stage. It was all one thing.

Q. How did these experiences change you?
A. I became more trusting of Source. I understood that behaviors that didn't support me could be shifted, that if I was called to be my most expansive self (we are all called in this way), then I was responsible for creating this expansion. The more I attuned to my divinity and my reason for being, the more expansive I became because there is no limit to how God can show up.

Q. What has been the most challenging part of your path?
A. It is walking the walk of evolution and understanding that it's just a process. If I judge where I am and what I'm going through, then it's painful. But if I step away and move into witness mode, then I look at my life as an evolution of spirit in which everything—good news or interesting news—becomes part of my growth. For example, I went through a highly visible and painful divorce. At the time, my ex-husband was doing a film and his billboards were all over Los Angeles. One day, I was on my way to church when I turned off the freeway and saw a new billboard of his. I screamed out loud, "Why me?" This quiet little voice said, "Because you are to see the God in him." When I heard that, I stopped and thought, *Oh my goodness. My judgment is keeping us locked together in a way that's not positive. So, if I stop judging him and start looking for the good in him, I will free us both.*

Q. What changes are you noticing about your life and the world?
A. It's that I don't have to do anything. My job is simply to show up and be available for Spirit—to be as prepared as I can for where Spirit guides me, as opposed to forcing, pushing, and controlling my life. If I really allow myself to be in the flow of

the divine, then it's much bigger, more powerful, and more effortless than anything I could create.

Q. What changes are others noticing about you?
A. They say I'm a totally different person. I have a friend who has known me for thirty years and she says she has witnessed me going from a caterpillar to a butterfly. I have become clearer and more open, communicative, and loving. I'm grateful for these changes because the "old me" felt like life was scary and that I had to fight to protect myself. A lot of that comes from my childhood. To move past that and trust that I'm guided and live in a safe universe is miraculous.

Q. What is your earliest memory? Why do you remember it?
A. My earliest memory is of sitting on my uncle's lap when I was two years old. I remember him talking to me and I felt loved and beautiful. My uncle and I are still really close. The funniest memory I have is of competing in a posture contest in eighth grade. I wore this yellow swimsuit and I was skinny and hadn't developed breasts yet. So my mother bought these little pads to go inside my suit so I would look proportionate. I looked great and won the contest. Afterwards, I kept the pads in and went swimming with the other kids. The pads popped out in the water. It was a pivotal moment because it was the first time I became aware of my image in the world.

Q. Who are your mentors? What have you learned from them?
A. Michael Beckwith. He's been my minister, teacher, and friend for thirty years. What Michael did was model complete trust in the absolute, that beyond all appearance, God is present. When I trust that, everything flows. Maya Angelou. Her creativity, presence, authenticity, and willingness to write and speak her truth have had great impact on me. Oprah Winfrey. She has been a conduit for change in the media by creating a platform for authors, speakers, and teachers to serve as healers in the world. There was a time when people tried

to pull her in another direction that was out of integrity with her soul and she said, "No." Now she is one of the most influential people in the country. Watching her taught me to ask, "Am I willing to stand in the integrity of my soul at any cost?"

Q. What is the greatest challenge facing society?

A. The greatest challenge is that we are asleep. We forget that we are connected and that our choices affect the whole. We must remember oneness because it is lack of remembrance that causes some of the catastrophic things we are experiencing. We see these catastrophes when countries, organizations, and individuals try to take care of their own little plot with regard to the larger impact.

Q. Are we waking up to oneness?

A. Yes and no. I see the greatest outpouring of hunger for health, well-being, and clarity that the planet has ever experienced. At the same time, I see the old paradigm fighting for its life more profoundly than ever. We are watching them happen simultaneously.

Q. What advice would you give someone just starting his or her spiritual path?

A. I would ask, "What is your intention?" This is important because intention seeds. I would then ask, "How willing are you to commit?" This helps the person see the difference between saying he or she wants something and doing what is necessary to obtain it.

Q. Please share an example of willingness to commit to something.

A. For me, it was acting. A lot of people want to be actors. Many of them have a need to be seen or validated. I knew I had talent but there was a moment when I realized, *I can't rely on raw talent. I have to invest in becoming skilled.* That's when I started taking advanced classes and performing in large venues. I wanted to become an actress I could be proud of.

Q. What are your practices for connecting to your higher purpose?

A. I read, do breath work, and go for walks in nature. I pray a lot during the day. I have an altar at home and here in my office at Mile Hi Church. I always have a little saying or affirmation that becomes my mantra for the day.

Q. How do you use these practices when you get out of balance?

A. Balance is something that is perpetually in motion. Every day, I ask, *Am I meditating and doing my spiritual practice? Am I getting enough rest? Am I exercising and eating well? Am I connecting with my family, friends, and husband?* There's an interweaving that goes on. When I find I am doing one of these things eighty percent of the time, then I know I am out of balance.

Q. Does one of your activities pull you out of balance more than others?

A. Ministry. It's not a one-day-a-week job. I am called to ministry because I am called to be of service. Service can look like being in my office, speaking on a platform, or performing a wedding ceremony. Sometimes it's counseling someone in crisis or working with women in prison. So the big place for me to create balance is remembering that ministry is not the totality of my life.

Q. Is this a challenge for many who are called to serve?

A. Light workers on the planet are struggling with this issue because there is a need to support health and well-being for humanity. It's a draw that pulls us. At the same time, we still have this human experience called wife, mother, sister, and friend. It takes consciousness to find a balance. Otherwise it is easy to drift into a less harmonious place.

Q. Have you ever felt weighed down by the world's pains?

A. No. I have felt sadness at our inhumanity and disappointed with our unwillingness to care for everyone, especially our women and children. But the weight doesn't belong to me. If you get that God is real, then you show up the best way you can every day to bring peace, love, and joy. But if you take on the weight of the world, then you have moved off the path of peace and what you have come here to do. It's because in that moment you have invested in separation. We are human, so we have these feelings. But the more we can move our attention—and intention—away from what is wrong to how we can contribute, then the more wholeness we can bring.

Q. How do you balance planning with remaining open to opportunity?
A. I'm pretty good at organizing my calendar and engagements. The way I manage on the spiritual level is to wait for an invitation. Because I know when I try to force something, it creates stress. But when I wait for the invitation, the perfect one comes at the perfect time.

Q. If you received $100,000, how would you spend it?
A. My mother is in a nursing home. So I would use part of it to create something to help her feel more beautiful, nurtured, and independent. I would use the rest to start a freedom camp for women who have been incarcerated. During a three-to-six-month intensive period, the women would contractually commit to learning how to take care of themselves and live in a more powerful place. They would learn health, well-being, spiritual practice, and work skills.

Q. If you had thirty seconds with someone in an elevator, what three things would you tell the person to do to be joyful, peaceful, and whole?
A. I would tell them to love themselves first, live a life of passion, and remember that service to humanity is why we are here.

Q. What books or resources have helped you the most? Why?

A. What has helped me is what I would recommend to others. I would encourage people to ask themselves daily, *Who am I and how can I serve?* I would invite them to create a weekly Sabbath, a day that they commit to having downtime, being nurtured, and doing what they love. I would ask them to take a five-day retreat once a year to meditate, rest, and spend time alone so they can connect to the still small voice. I would tell them not to fear going into places where they feel scared or overwhelmed because going into that energy is a portal to healing.

Q. What would you like to be written on your tombstone?
A. I'm not sure about a tombstone, but I know how I'd like to be remembered. I would like people to celebrate my legacy—my commitment to God, humanity, and being a transformative agent. I believe that life is eternal, so I would step into the next dimension with light, joy, and grace.

Q. Anything else?
A. I would like us to pay attention to our young people. There are many children who are extraordinarily gifted and connected. They are wisdom carriers who sometimes have a hard time being on the planet because of our discordant energy. If we pay attention to these light beings, they will remind us of who we are and what we have come here to be.

"Pain by itself is merely pain, but the experience of pain coupled with an understanding that the pain serves a worthy purpose is suffering. Suffering is meaningful. Suffering can be endured because there is a reason for it that is worth the effort. What is more worthy of your pain than the evolution of your soul?"

-Gary Zukav

Reprinted with the permission of Simon & Schuster, Inc., from SEAT OF THE SOUL by Gary Zukav. Copyright © 1989 by Gary Zukav. All rights reserved.

15

"Let pain have its way with you."
Lisa Jones, Best Selling Author and Journalist

Lisa Jones has been a journalist for twenty-six years. She has written about the environment, food, and the Miss Navajo Beauty Pageant for publications like the *New York Times* magazine, *Smithsonian*, and *High Country News*. She lives in Colorado with her husband and cat. *Broken: A Love Story*, the story of her friendship with quadriplegic Northern Arapaho horse gentler and traditional healer Stanford Addison, is her first book. Her website is www.lisajoneswrites.com.

Q. What experiences put you on your spiritual path?
A. Starting to fail in the realms I knew—work, Presbyterianism, being liked and popular—all that status and achievement stuff. It had worked for a long time and then it didn't work anymore. I was tripping over my own well-disguised wound of not trusting people, especially men. So in my mid-thirties, I went from being the belle of the ball to feeling like an alienated weirdo. Everyone was getting married and having kids. I thought, *Of course, I'll do that. I get everything I want from men.* But it didn't work, mostly because I didn't know how to relax, commit, and forgive people. I was carrying around a lot of stuff. In my own eyes, I became a failure as I dropped out of my editing job, my engagement to be married, and my owning a home. I ended up working in a Buddhist meditation center[2] as a cook and secretary for a year. It was fantastic. I recommend it even to those who do not need to take a massive personal growth step. It is just so great to take time off and not be important, to just be a helper.

---

[2] Lisa Jones worked at the Insight Meditation Society's Retreat Center in Barre, Massachusetts headed by Sharon Salzberg.

My stay there followed eight months of deep depression. Being there got me on the path. The Buddhist path was the obvious one for me. It is so accepting and nonjudgmental. I never went back to being a full-time salaried, health-insured yuppie. I worked less and had more time for spiritual practices such as meditation retreats. I also was doing better with men. At least I was going for the softies, men who valued softness in themselves and others.

After five years of mellowing out, I got a lead on a story about this great horse trainer named Stanford Addison. I was forty-two when I went up on this assignment and saw Stanford, who knocked me silly the minute I met him. I knew instantly, *Oh boy, you're toast. This guy sees right through you.* I have never had an experience like that before. I had been with some great Buddhist teachers, mostly Western, but a few Tibetans, and had never felt that. I was in a bigger container—a big pot of stew—and something molecular was about to change. I was terrified, but also deeply thrilled.

I stayed there only four days the first time. I ended up gentling—or let's just say riding—a horse. I had a very climactic experience in the coral. The horse threw me at one point and I flew in the air and landed on my feet. I wasn't really in my body to experience that but that was pretty much a metaphor for what was about to happen in a bigger way. Something about Stanford was not consensual. It was cellular and chemical. It was like, "Here you go. You can leave and not do this but . . ." In retrospect, I have this wisdom about it. At the time, I was like "What am I doing? I can't stop thinking about him. I'm going back to my regular life but there is this other thing that is really big up there."

It took me nine months to finally go back up. When I did, there was this tension of opposites. My life is so comfortable here and it's so not comfortable up there. Yet I'm more comfortable on the reservation, even though every time I cross through those differences, there is always that feeling of going into the unknown, the uncomfortable, and the unpredictable. Here in white suburbia, I can predict every day. There, I can't even predict the events of one day. It was complete surrender and wonder at its best. Just two weeks ago I was up there, seven years after I met Stan, and again, there was that surrender and wonder. It's a whole other world. I do have a feeling it is coming to some sort of resolution or ending now.

Q. How did these experiences change you?
A. I have changed in a psychological way. I was a nice house built on a crappy foundation. The foundation was crappy because I didn't trust men. I grew up with a strange father and developed some weird boundaries with men. I invited disrespect in a way that wasn't obvious but was definitely there. Stanford is so much more powerful than me. Even though we are friends now, it is not a relationship of equals. Before his accident, he was a big womanizer, and yet he always treated me with immaculate respect. It was like medicine. I needed respect so badly and I didn't even know it. It couldn't have worked with an ordinary person, someone from my own culture I felt equal to. It had to be someone so much more powerful that I could be the child and he could be the daddy. I felt that powerless on the reservation, that innocent and small. He made my foundation whole without moving the house. I don't know how he did it. He must be a great carpenter! That's the main change. Four years after meeting Stan, I married Peter, my husband. It's a good marriage, the right choice. So that's a huge change too.

Another amazing thing was that I finally allowed myself to be quiet. Even though we yak and tell stories, I've noticed that as the years have gone on, I've become quieter. I just want to help out and do what needs to be done. Part of it is that I'm finished with the book. When I was writing it, a huge spiritual and psychological thing was happening to me and I wanted it. Now, as my friend Ciska says, "You're full. You're done feasting on that." That's true. But before, regardless of whether the book was done or not, I still would have made sure I was the center of attention. Now I don't care. It's the hugest relief to an extroverted, competitive middle child like me. I just want to make sure Stan has enough breakfast or protein to keep his blood sugar steady and that he knows I'm here in case he needs me. I am happy to be of service. It's a natural thing. I wasn't like, "Okay, this is the next step." I just don't need to say a whole lot. Sometimes I think, *Should I open my mouth? Can I improve on this silence?* Then, I think, *No. I'll just close it.*

At one reading somebody asked, "Are you a shaman?" I said, "No. I am so not a shaman." I'm not particularly enlightened, wise, or free of ego but I am a happier person—a lot happier. And I'm a lot more "let go." I have an intimate relationship with wonder and joy. But I'm not like Stanford. That's a great thing because he still helps me a lot. It's easy to fall off and I have to learn lessons every day. Each time I go to that dark place, I have to relearn how to be there and endure it for a while and then let it fall away. I have to relearn this all the time. But every time I am with Stan, I get straightened out in some way.

There is no way to go up to the reservation and not have your dark material show up because we're afraid, indoctrinated, and guilty. It's really an exercise in being able to endure those things and somehow still navigate. It's a very concentrated slice of life for any white person sensitive to what they are feeling. Some of my friends who have been there don't want to go back because it's just too much.

I will always go back. It's not only a personal spiritual experience, but also an experience of facing what it is to be American—what it means to live on Arapahoe Road, ski at Arapahoe Basin, and attend Arapahoe High School. What that word means, who those people are, and where we put them—up there and in Oklahoma. I'm not saying let's hate ourselves and go back to Europe. I'm just saying there's a shadow side to being American. I think that's why Native Americans are so invisible in our culture. Who wants to think about that?

Q. What changes are you noticing about your life and the world?
A. I believe in magic now. I'm certainly not an expert, but I don't reject it anymore. I have this feeling of parallel universes. Like when I am driving and see something in the middle of the road and think, *Oh my God, that's a newborn black calf!* Then it turns out to be an old coat or garbage bag. And I think to myself, *You know, that could have been a calf that flashed in for a second and decided to turn into a garbage bag.* I'm not brain damaged, but I do ask questions like, "Who knows if trees can hear what we say?" I feel as though I don't really know anything. That might be part of aging. You get to where you are like, "The truth? I don't know." I'm not nearly as certain as I used to be. I know that the linear, visible, post-industrial mechanical view of the universe that our culture holds up is not the last word. So that's changed. It's fun to have these thoughts.

Q. Have you always had a sense of humor or did that come out more on the reservation?
A. No, I've always been funny and that is one reason it worked for me up there. Those guys have a great sense of humor. People who know different Native American tribes often say, "The Arapahos are really funny." Stan said, "If we didn't laugh, we'd cry." His family, in particular, has a dynamite sense of humor. Stan uses it to put you at ease. Sometimes people say, "You are so brave. You keep going up to that place." Actually, I'm having such a good time. I laugh my head off and relax so much up there. So it's not like I'm a noble person saying, "I'll suffer to get this message out." I have a blast and get fed in a lot of ways. Of course, they tease me to bits sometimes, but that is okay.

Q. What has been the most challenging part of your path?
A. The hardest part was seeing this other world. Stanford was showing me another reality and I felt like Alice in Wonderland. At one point, I thought I was losing my mind. That was scary. It was also hard that my life in Paonia, Colorado, was chugging along like normal. I would take these strange voyages to Wyoming and come back with my eyes wide like pie plates. It was two distinct, separate worlds. I felt lonely because I was wrestling with stuff that no one else on my block was. My husband was really great. He came up with me a few times, as did my mother and some other friends. That really helped. But in the beginning, my worlds were not integrated. I would listen to my white, middle-class friends and think, *This is so boring. There is a whole other world out there.* I felt like a crazy astronaut who didn't know what to say.

It's hard being a bridge person—being between two worlds. I didn't feel like I had a tribe of my own. It was also hard introducing my friends up there and trying to integrate the two. Actually, it was exhausting watching everyone go through the first few steps of incredulity, enchantment, and fear. When talking to them about it, I thought, *Oh my God, I am so tired.* It made me a grumpier person. I'm pretty extroverted and this was a solitary thing. So it was challenging to not have those tribes merging. Now that the book is over, it's happened.

Q. What changes are others noticing about you?
A. Stanford said a really nice thing to a reporter from *The Denver Post*. She asked, "How has Lisa changed?" He said something like, "She used to be too accommodating. Now she is just a really comfortable person." It's a very nice thing to say, the highest praise. Yeah, I feel pretty comfortable. I feel confident with the book because I worked hard not to make proclamations about Native people and keep it really personal. I am confident of the material and of my conclusions.

Q. What is the greatest challenge facing society?
A. I'll focus on America. We are in love with affluence and productivity, partly because we are so afraid of the apocalypse, which is coming due to our environmental, economic, trade, and health care practices. We externalize our apocalypses, turning them on others such as the Native Americans, people in the Middle East, and whoever else pisses us off. So we are scrambling up a slippery slope and we have been since we founded this country.

These guys on the reservation live a post-apocalyptic lifestyle and it's not that bad. I think we are going to find this out for ourselves. It might be preferable to live in a tiny three bedroom house with eleven people rather than a 3,500 square-foot house with only our spouse and all kinds of gadgets… and a big huge alarm system so nobody takes our gadgets. I think we are destroying the planet in order to avoid this kind of poverty, to avoid having to share when there is not enough. The great lesson of these guys is that it can be fun to live with eleven people and not have that much stuff and sit and pray together twice a week. When was the last time white middle-class people did that? In the Middle Ages or the Agricultural Era? I'm not trying to romanticize it because it is really hard too. But the idea that we need to bust down the next frontier to have our space, it's just not that happy making. We are moving toward things that do not bring us joy. Not that we should live in poverty. But it might not be bad to live densely and share a vibrant spiritual life.

I was on a panel once with other Native American expert types. One man was talking about the Native plight. I said, "That's true. But we should really look at our own plight and see how they have held on to things we lost centuries ago, such as extended families, praying together, and helping each other out in a real way." They still have interdependence. They need each other. We're such individuals and pioneers that it can be pretty damn lonely. They are lots of things, but they are not lonely.

It is violent on the reservation, though. Young men die violent deaths and there is lots of addiction. I'm not saying these things are good, but I do think somewhere deep in my soul, it's a more accurate representation of the human condition. We live in a bubble here in white America. It's a delusional thing because you go anywhere else and you see violence and death. I value life a lot more now that I have seen so much of it end.

The other thing that is eye-opening is their quick transition from joy to sorrow, back to joy. At funerals, people scream at the sky. Thank God someone is screaming. Why would we be polite after a seventeen-year-old kid gets stabbed in the heart? It isn't a time to be restrained. But then they laugh. They bear so much loss, and yet they're still together, still laughing.

When we experience loss, it's private and therapeutic. They are so communalized that they just feel stuff. For example, we'll be talking and someone will say, "Well, you know that time she did that." I'll ask, "What time when who did what?" But they all know. It's a lack of intelligence on my part that I don't. How much of this is unspoken? Or they will say, "Someone is coming." I'll ask, "When?" Then in ten minutes someone shows up, but the person was two miles away when they said he or she was coming. How is this possible? Do they share a brain? There is something really intimate about it.

Q. What advice would you give someone just starting his or her spiritual path?
A. A woman at one of my readings said, "How do I find a shaman?" My feeling was, "Don't look in the brightly lit places. Keep your mind open when you are in the more shadowy, less privileged spots. The world is full of wisdom and I don't

think it is in the brightly lit places. What worked for me was letting pain have its way with me and following my heart. If you let pain have its way with you, your heart opens. Nature abhors a vacuum. I never want to sound like I know what other people should do because I don't. Maybe the "win friends and influence people" folks are right. I don't know. I have never been to their seminars. When Stan happened to me, it was like being hit with a bludgeon. It was not, "Hmm, should I try this out?" Sometimes things hit you pretty hard, and you just know they are right. Or at least they're the next step. When I see things like *The Secret*, I have to ask, "Who funded that book, the Republican Party (joking)? We are just a bunch of dying animals.

When I first went to the Buddhist meditation center, there was a community of twenty-five people living there. Someone said, "Why are you here?" I replied, "Oh, I left my job and got dumped by my fiancé. I'll never have a husband. My life is over." He said, "Oh yeah, that's why everyone comes." I said, "Really, that's fantastic!" He said, "People come through the door suffering. They don't come because everything is great." However, it does feel like some people aren't in pain at all, like my brother-in-law Jamie. We joke about it saying, "Then, there's Jamie's pain body. Ha ha, he doesn't have one!"

Q. What are your practices for connecting to your higher purpose?
A. Peter and I were such Buddhists together. We would go on these long retreats. Then I got into Stan. As I say in my book, *Broken: A Love Story*, it was hot up there and it's cool in Buddhism. I wanted heat. There was something broken in me that needed welding. Now I'm into Buddhism again but I don't have a daily practice.

Writing the book was a big practice. I had all those experiences up there. We were sweating all the time. Sweat lodges are intense, long ceremonies that can be physically painful. So I was like, I am done with that. Now I am going to go write the book. But writing it was another excruciating experience—to actually look at what happened, write it down, and own it. I had to write the assault scene five times for my writing group. I thought, *I am going to shoot myself if I have to think about it anymore.* There were also long conversations on the phone with Stan asking questions and fleshing things out. The act of writing is amazing because it makes you own it. It is so easy to misspeak. But when you miswrite, you know it.

So that was my spiritual practice and it just recently ended. I still go up to Stan's a lot and sweat. Now it's become clear that I can use a little Buddhism to even things out. The coolness, gentleness, and safety are desirable to me. That was a pretty damn hot furnace I was in. I'm exhausted.

Actually, I have been exhausted for the last couple of weeks. I was worried about my health. Then I thought, *What if you just embraced it, surrendered to it, which is the whole story of Stan's life, Buddhism, and every spiritual path worth its salt?* So I got on the couch and started reading novels. I said, "God, I'm in heaven." There is so much good about being exhausted.

I actually was going to go on a Buddhist retreat in September, but I have too many events right now, so I can't do it. But my fantasy is to go away on silent retreat and just sit. Not necessarily meditate, just sit and let it all go. I feel so blessed to have all these resources. My husband is a Buddhist meditation teacher and I can say to him, "Give me a dharma talk right now on surrender," and he'll do it, which is really great because he's so good at it. He'd also say, "Oh my God, that's the sexiest thing I've ever heard!" He's a bit of a Thomas Merton. I'm not saying, "The Buddha wasn't good enough for me so I had to go to a modern day shaman." The Buddha is great. All paths are great. I just happen to have this intense, personal connection with Stan. Somehow it worked for both of us.

Q. What books or resources have helped you the most? Why?
A. The poet Rainer Maria Rilke is often criticized for being a big, fat downer. But I love Rilke and often read poetry when my life is a big, fat downer. Rilke knows this territory well, as his mother used to dress him up like a little girl. His really famous pieces are the *Duino Elegies* and *Letters to a Young Poet*, but I just found a poem called "The Man Watching." It has a stanza that says, "When we win it's with small things, / and the triumph itself makes us small. / What is extraordinary and eternal / does not want to be bent by us." We're talking about a German guy saying this, not a Tibetan or Native American or someone from a more "let go" culture. These words bring me a lot of peace when I am feeling powerless and miserable and trying to make everyone see that being with someone like Stan is a great path.

So I have been reading a lot of Rilke . . . and Leonard Cohen. There's a concert film called *I'm Your Man* that's about Cohen. In it, a guy named Antony sings a song called, "If It Be Your Will," which has exactly the same theme as the Rilke poem. That song brings me to tears. Having things like this available is so helpful. I don't have to go to Nepal or the Indian reservation or church to get it. It's right there on the Internet.

My all-time favorite T.S. Eliot poem is "Ash Wednesday" with the lines, "Suffer me not to be separated / And let my cry come unto Thee." If Native sweat lodges picked a quote from English literature that best exemplified their experience that would be it. Because in the lodge, people cry, suffer, and emote. And it's going somewhere. It's being shared. I love T.S. Eliot. That guy really knew how to suffer. His *Four Quartets* poems are great too.

These are my touchstones. Just being open to the human experience by returning to a favorite poet or going out with friends helps me touch inward and gives me what I need.

Q. Anything else?
A. There is so much to be learned from Stanford's example. He is a wonderful model of what it means to be a spiritual leader. Stanford had every possible thing taken from him, short of his life. He was a gorgeous, strong horseman, a womanizer, and a karate expert who played guitar in a band. You can't imagine a more vibrant, sexy young guy. Then, at age twenty, he was struck down in a car accident and couldn't move anything. He had his head screwed into a board. The subsequent health consequences of being quadriplegic are horrendous. Just to be Native American is hard enough, but Stanford's had everything taken from him. It's biblical what happened to him. In the hospital, they gave him hormones to treat his spinal cord injury, which caused him to break out in boils. To address that, they gave him more medicine that caused his teeth to fall out. It was a cascading effect of "we are going to take it all from you."

Think about Jesus Christ. He was crucified for only a day or two. Stan has been in this unreliable body for thirty years now—and he's still pretty calm, happy, and comfortable with himself. He devotes every waking minute to serving people. Just being near that is like, "Whoa!" It's sincere. He takes phone calls all night long from people in terrible situations.

Stanford's story is one of ego death. He does not aggrandize, narcotize, or serve his own ego in any way. He is just trying to help. His modeling this opened possibilities for me. I was so conditioned and so quasi-successful that I couldn't imagine serving any god other than the god of achievement. He is one of the best people I have ever met and he has lost everything. He doesn't piss and moan about it. He did for a while. He even tried to kill himself. Now his life is about showing that there's a way to be without all the stuff, without even a body that functions. His body functions just to keep his spirit alive, but it doesn't function for anything else.

I'm not saying everyone who has lost things is great because some people who have experienced loss are really bitter and scary and won't teach you anything. But you'd be surprised by the teachers you can find in the less privileged places.

"It's been said that the difference between all of us living at ordinary levels of human consciousness and those we call saints is that they never forget God even for a single moment. They're cheerful when life is difficult, patient when others are impatient, and loving when others respond with hatred."

-Dr. Wayne Dyer

Reprinted from The Essence of Being in Balance (2006) by Dr. Wayne Dyer with permission of Hay House, Inc., Carlsbad, CA. www.hayhouse.com.

"When we take a step towards grace, it takes 1,000 steps towards us."
Skip Lackey, Senior Journey Trainer and Practitioner, North America

Skip has been a close personal friend of Brandon Bays, founder of The Journey, for over twenty years and is mentioned in her book, *The Journey*, as one of the eight people who actively supported her during her healing journey. He staffed the first Journey Accreditation program, is a Senior Journey Practitioner, and the Senior Trainer for North America. For twenty-five years Skip worked as an actor, writer, director, and producer for film, stage, and television. His passion for diving into the core of human emotion has taken him down many paths. He is certified in Neuro-Linguistic Programming (NLP), Neuro-Associative Conditioning (NAC), and has studied numerous other healing modalities. He and his wife Kristine travel all over the U.S. and Canada, passionately sharing The Journey workshop events.

Q. What experiences put you on your spiritual path?
A. My mother studied astrology, mediation, and yoga when I was young. Her metaphysical interests eventually lead her to leave Catholicism and become a Buddhist. Through her influence, I began meditating at age eleven and learned Silva Mind Control and other advanced techniques. During my teenage years, I got interested in theater and wanted to go to Broadway. My dad didn't want me to because he was a tough, meat-and-potatoes kind of guy. He tried to shut me down, but I went anyway. When I got to New York City, I was cast in an Off-Broadway show in which I had to cry. The tears wouldn't come and I didn't understand why. So I started looking into emotional release work. I began taking different workshops, including the very first one Tony Robbins did.

Tony was twenty-four and I was twenty-three. In the workshop, he convinced me to walk across a bed of hot coals with him and I was completely blown away.

A while later, I left New York and drove out to Los Angeles to start a film and television career. I ended up studying Neuro-Linguistic Programming (NLP) with Tony and NLP founders Richard Bandler, Leslie LeBeau (formerly Leslie Cameron-Bandler), and John Grinder. That's where I met Brandon Bays, who was working with her husband as a trainer for Tony. She and I became good friends. I also got into different spiritual practices and became a master trainer in nutrition, hypnotherapy, meditation, and other areas.

Studying emotions as an actor opened me to my feelings. It was like unlocking Pandora's box. As I let go of physical and emotional traumas stored in my body, I got clearer and clearer. Then in my early thirties, I got a call from Brandon, who told me she had a uterine tumor the size of a small basketball. She was forming a healing group of trusted friends and asked if I would be part of it. I said, "Yes, of course." I had been doing NLP work with people who had tumors, but the results were hit or miss. Some healed and some didn't. I never really understood why. After doing emotional release work with this group, Brandon had a spontaneous healing in which her tumor went away in three-and-a-half weeks.

I went on to study nutrition with Dr. Timothy Brantley, author of *The Cure: Heal Your Body, Save Your Life*, and he and I became friends. Tim, Roy Sekoff (founding editor of *The Huffington Post*), and I would have long conversations about health and wellness, which taught me about how the body works.

I then went to film school because I had a desire to make movies with a positive message. During that time, my first marriage broke up and I went into a deep depression. Even with all my skills, I couldn't pull myself out of it. I reached out to a handful of friends, including Debra Angeletti who said, "You remember what happened to Brandon? She's created a process for other people to let go of emotional trauma. It sounds perfect for you." I had gone for months without being able to get off the floor. But after this conversation, I immediately flew to Los Angeles, where Debra did The Journey process with me. I literally saw the game of abandonment that had played out my whole life. How I pushed women away because of my insecurity, which I wasn't even aware of because it was on a deep, other than conscious, level. Ending my first marriage was actually my own doing, even though I blamed someone else. During The Journey process, I had access to deep wisdom. So I continued doing the work to find out what else was holding me back.

The Journey work not only helped me, but it also saved my older son. When my first wife was pregnant, her water broke at twenty-two weeks. The doctors said our son had less than ½ of a 1% chance of survival. We used The Journey techniques and my first wife's membranes healed over. The doctors said they had heard about that happening but they had never actually seen it. Since that time, I have helped many pregnant women with uterine infections and ruptured membranes heal.

After my older son was born, Brandon's book, *The Journey*, was getting ready to be released in the United Kingdom. She contacted me saying, "I've written about your role in my healing process. Is it okay to publish the information?" I said, "Absolutely, and I'd like to learn more about what you are doing." She came to New York and said, "Why don't you come over to England and see what we are doing?" I went over and did a few of her seminars. I was completely blown away. People were working at the deepest level possible to get at their emotional traumas, and some of them had no prior background in mind-body healing. And they had just as powerful an experience as those who had been doing this kind of work their entire lives. I started going back and forth between the U.S. and the U.K., helping Brandon with the business. I was learning the work and became the first practitioner in North America.

Then I had an experience that changed my life. One of the owners of the company I worked for (who was also a friend) came to me and said, "My fiancé's sixteen-year-old niece, Danielle, has been in a car crash. Is there anything you can do for her? She's in a coma with brain swelling and her organs are shutting down. They don't think she is going to make it." I replied, "I talk to people and help them release stored emotions. I haven't worked with anyone who is unable to speak." Then I remembered hearing about practitioners doing work with people in hospitals and I thought, *What the hell. What do I have to lose?* At least I can support my friend. When I went into Danielle's hospital room, the priest was walking out, having just given her Last Rites. Her parents said, "You are our last chance." I sat by her bed and was able to drop into a deep state of other-than-conscious-awareness to work with her. She had advanced respiratory distress syndrome (ARDS) from swallowing vomit that had created an infection in her lungs. After working with her, the ARDS went away in only forty-eight hours. The doctors had never seen that before. Another time, she nonverbally shared things about past traumas with me that her parents were able to confirm.

I thought I was going crazy because I was working in network sports broadcasting and had never done anything like this. But every time I worked with her, she had milestones. She ended up coming out of the coma, taking her first steps, and eventually dancing with me. She had a lot of brain damage because the swelling had been there for several weeks before we did The Journey work. But still, she was alive and dancing with support!

This experience changed my perception about what's possible. Afterwards, I started working with other nonverbal clients—babies, coma patients—and was able to connect with them in the same way. But I couldn't explain what was happening, so that frightened me. Yet I also knew it was my calling.

What I have learned from years of doing Journey work is that it's about stopping and facing our deepest fears. When we go back and release these blocks, the body rises up to meet the challenge. It's like that saying, "When we take one step towards grace, grace takes 1,000 steps towards us." When people take steps towards healing themselves, the universe comes rushing in saying, "I get it. You are committed. Now let's do it." For example, I had pain in my neck for years after an accident. After one Journey process in which I remembered and released a near drowning experience, my body was able to heal itself. When we clear trauma, it's amazing what the body can do.

This past year, all these books have come out about emotional healing. It's the work Brandon has been doing since the early 1990s but back then, it was difficult to get people to walk down this path because they were so afraid of their emotions. Emotions are the gateway to the soul, to Source, to all healing. People just need to open up and let themselves feel what's there.

Q. What changes are you noticing about your life and the world?
A. I spent some time in India doing a yātrā or spiritual journey some years ago. It was a life changing experience. Here in North America, we have everything and yet we are still searching for what we lack—happiness and wholeness. In India, there are the haves and the have-nots. But what amazed me was that the have-nots spend time being thankful for the little things they do have.

When I went over there, I was overwhelmed by both the poverty and love of the people. In the U.S., people use the term *"namaste"* loosely, but in parts of India, it is said with great reverence five hundred times a day. The people over there just want to connect.

This experience gave me great compassion. Most of us are in our own private hell trying to figure out how to survive. We can thrive if we can just be present and have compassion for what's going on around us. People get so caught up in their daily lives that they lose sight of our interconnectedness. One of the traumas I had to clear with The Journey was my father's being killed in an airplane disaster. My dad was a salesman who spoke to everyone. I remember asking him as a teenager, "Why are you always talking to everybody?" He said, "I believe that everyone who crosses my path has something to teach me. So I ask questions until I find out what it is." I never forgot that. It wasn't until years later when I found myself doing the same thing that I really got what he meant. Life is about being in the moment.

In the movie, *The Adventures of Buckaroo Banzai Across the 8th Dimension*, Buckaroo Banzai says, "No matter where you go, there you are." He means, wherever you are at, be there, be present. That's when all joy is at your disposal. If joy is not there, then bring it. You be the joy. Or as Gandhi said, "Be the change you wish to see in the world." Resting in that is contagious.

The older I get, the more I realize I don't know. There is such mystery and excitement in seeing things unfold. Science is now proving what people have been doing for millennia with consciousness, wholeness, and healing. It's an exciting time as we awaken to oneness.

Q. When people trigger us, how can we remain in love instead of responding negatively?

A. When you know you are going to say or do something you'll regret, it's best to remove yourself from the situation. Then ask, "What's inside me that's getting triggered? What's here that I'm supposed to learn?" We can't change other people, but we can change ourselves. And when our consciousness shifts, so does theirs. With The Journey, we teach you how to identify these cell memories from childhood and clear them. This process is especially helpful for those issues that hook you over and over again, causing endless cycles of pain and shutdown.

Q. What has been the most challenging part of your path?
A. Knowing in my gut what's supposed to happen and having my mind kick in with doubts. So time goes by where I don't take that step toward doing what I know is inevitable. There have been times when I've put myself to sleep because the idea of stepping forward scared the crap out of me. I say this even though I have taken some big risks during which the universe supported me. But the hardest thing is taking that first step.

Q. What is your earliest memory? Why do you remember it?
A. In The Journey, we go beyond the conscious mind to tap into memories that are stored at a deeper level. I've had memories of things that I didn't consciously recall but when I asked my mom about them, she verified them, time and time again. I do remember my mother and father fighting a lot and being in and out of their relationship. During my first Journey process, I realized I had bought into this idea of abandonment. Letting go of that allowed me to stop pushing people away.

I also remember being six or seven years old and feeling spiritually connected to God. I asked God for help and when I felt I wasn't being heard, I shut off. Then there was this longing to reconnect. But it wasn't until I started doing Journey work that I realized my connection had always been there. When I got back into that flow, everything started to happen.

Q. Who are your mentors? What have you learned from them?
A. I learned a lot from Dr. Tim Brantley and Tony Robbins. I also learned a lot about speaking the truth from my acting teacher Sanford (Sandy) Meisner. He and Lee Strasberg were the two living masters and I had the privilege of studying with Sandy for two years. But my greatest teachers have been the individuals with whom I have done Journey work. Every single person that I have worked with has taught me about the possibilities of the human spirit. This keeps me humble. I've had a lot of teachers, but I think these are the ones who have had the greatest impact.

Q. What is the greatest challenge facing society?
A. In the U.S., we created a set of rules that serve as a social contract. But where did these rules come from? And what purpose do they serve? Some of them limit us even though our motto is "Land of the Free, Home of the Brave." And most of us don't realize that we are truly free at our core. We want to make different decisions but we don't because we get caught up in society's or our parent's rules. I'm not talking about anarchy. I'm talking about being able to be everything we want to be as opposed to keeping up with the Jones. If everybody threw that out the window and followed their passion, what would happen, who couldn't we be? That's the real question.

I go back and forth between breaking free and getting caught up in the rules. Sometimes it's easier to follow them and other times, I step outside and say, "No, this rule doesn't make sense." We can avoid this by using the Socratic method to ask, "Why is this like this? Does it serve us?" The great leaders are constantly challenging their perceptions saying, "How can I look at this differently? Where's the opportunity?" There's no, "This is the way it has always been so this is the way we're going to do it." That type of thinking stops us from stepping into our greatness.

The Journey team recognized the need for this type of leadership so we started a new organization called Conscious Company Worldwide. Through it, we teach people how to live in authenticity, truth, and passion so they can make a difference. We're even training tribal elders and teachers in aboriginal communities so they can mentor troubled youth. For example, I worked with an aboriginal group in Canada called Natuashish that has a suicide rate ten to twelve times higher than any other native group in Canada. The results were so awesome that the chief invited us to come back.

Q. What are your practices for connecting to your higher purpose and how do you use them when you get out of balance?
A. I had another teacher named Papaji. I never met him in body but I started seeing visions of him and have been to his ashram in India several times. His book, *The Truth Is*, changed my life. In it, he said something like, "Call off the search. You are what you seek. There's nothing outside of you. When people wake up to this consciousness, it happens in an instant. So why can't that instant be right now?" When I read this, it reaffirmed my desire to stop searching and go within.

I also studied with another teacher named Gurumayi who taught me the mantra, "*Om Nama Shivaya*." So many people have chanted this over the years that as soon as I say it, my stress and anxiety just melt away. It's like a doorway to welcoming whatever I feel so it can come and go. It's only when I push my feelings away that they come roaring back.

Life goes by quickly. So I wake up every day being thankful and meditate when I need to. I always try to maintain gratitude and humility, knowing that if life really gets me down, I always have access to The Journey process. The Journey allows me to let go of traumas like my divorce and my father's death so they don't run my life. It enables me to see that it all starts with me. I can't control others' actions but I can say, "Okay, they are angry. They are living life the way they need to. And I can choose to forgive." Anger leads to sickness and shutdown.

Q. How do you balance planning with remaining open to opportunity?
A. This is one of my greatest challenges. It's our mission to help people open to possibility. In living this mission, I sometimes feel out of balance. Last summer, I was on a vision quest in Saskatchewan and saw an image of my wife Kristine and me having another baby. (Kristine and I have a daughter. I also have my son from my first marriage.) I called her and said, "We have to talk about something." She said, "I know. It's about our having another baby." We had both gotten the same message and tried to push it away. But it came up again during another vision quest so we said, "Okay," and conceived on the first try.

So with the baby on the way, we're training more people to do the initial Journey Intensive Workshop so I can focus on developing strategy, teaching the advanced courses, and spending time with my family. As far as balancing each day, we spend forty-five minutes each morning meditating and talking about what needs to get done. We also have our staff go through The Journey courses so they are grounded in the work. We try to walk our talk and when we work too hard, we find ourselves getting triggered. I'm not saying I've got all the answers. Each of us knows what's best for us. What's right for me is recognizing when I'm overextended and taking measures to bring myself back into balance.

Q. If you received $100,000, how would you spend it?
A. I'd give some to the five orphanages we sponsor in India. Ravi, the gentleman who runs them, is a saint. We are putting him through our outreach program so he can do Journey work with the kids. Here in North America, I'd fund a program in a predominantly Hispanic school in Colorado and continue our work with the aboriginal community in Canada. We are

creating a nonprofit organization to support more of these programs because I know we can make a huge difference.

In the interest of balance, I'd use some of the money to pay off my mortgage. I serve so much, I sometimes need to step back and say, "Okay, it's time to take care of myself." Brandon and her husband also give one hundred percent. The last few years, they have been taking more vacation time and now I'm starting to do that too. But our mission is always there.

Q. If you had thirty seconds with someone in an elevator, what three things would you tell the person to do to be joyful, peaceful, and whole?
A. I'd smile, make a heartfelt connection, and tell them to have a wonderful day. Sometimes people's suffering overwhelms me. That's how I felt when I visited a small town in the Himalayas. After seeing the poverty there, I went back to my hotel and cried. I had to really look at what was showing up for me and say, "This is their path. Be present and connect with them." The minute I started doing that, I realized that's all they really wanted. They wanted a heartfelt connection.

Q. What books or resources have helped you the most? Why?
A. Read *The Journey*, by Brandon Bays. The people who read it call our office crying at the possibilities. Read *The Biology of Belief*, by Bruce Lipton. That book explains how consciousness affects the body in an accessible way. Read *The Cure*, by Tim Brantley. It's a great book on nutrition. Any book on alkalizing the body to aid self-healing is a good resource.

The book *The Truth Is*, by Papaji is mind blowing. It takes me so deep into the possibility of truth that I can read only two or three pages at a time. When you read the book, you may not understand it at first but keep going. Eventually, it will start to penetrate and quiet your mind.

I also like doing *kirtan* chanting. Krishna Das, the chanting musician, was recently in town and Kristine and I attended his concert for our anniversary. Chanting *kirtans* is a beautiful way to suspend everything and pray singing, "God is good, life is great," in different languages. I also think doing a daily practice is helpful. You can meditate, take a walk, spend time in nature, read about consciousness, or listen to music—whatever. Just take some time to be with yourself.

Q. What would you like to be written on your tombstone or said about you after you die?

A. I want to be cremated and have my ashes spread somewhere. I know that when my journey in this body ends, there will be something else. I have felt it when working with people who are dying. So if I were to die tomorrow, I wouldn't have any regrets. I have been living my mission and have left nothing unsaid.

Two ideas come to mind in contemplating what people would say about me. First, Gurumayi often used the term *"seva,"* or selfless service. I hope people would say that I lived in selfless service. Second, when my dad died, fifteen hundred people came to his funeral. Some came to our house with food and said things like, "I work at the gas station. Your dad felt like a friend. His passing is a great loss to me." This outpouring made a huge impression on me. My dad worked from home, yet his life touched so many. Although he and I had a rocky relationship early on, he taught me much about human connection and eventually became one of my best friends. My life is about staying humble, connecting with others, and practicing *seva*.

Q. Anything else?

A. The universe gives you gifts all the time, but if you are not clear inside, or if your intention is too narrow, you might miss them. How many of us have said, "I really want this." and a little voice inside said, *Who do you think you are? You can't have that!* Those are the cell memories stored in your body. They're little saboteurs that yank you off your goals. We have a whole course on abundance that is about how to clear these memories. Once you clear them, you can truly ask and receive.

I wrote an article a few months ago that was published in *Metaphysical Journey*. It was about a spiritual teacher in India saying, "Expectation is an invitation to hell." When I heard this, my whole body started convulsing. I realized that when we have expectations, we try to hit a bull's-eye. Often times, we hit all around it, but since we don't hit the point we intend, we get disappointed. But the universe is saying, "Yeah, but look what you got over here, and here, and here." But we don't get the message because we are stuck on one thing. We almost never hit our expectations exactly. So if we don't accept the universe's gifts, we'll always be disappointed.

What works better is saying, "Here's my intention. I'll accept what's given." That's wisdom. Follow that path. Because what you think you want is always mixed with mind and ego—and those can lead you astray. It took me years of working with people to get this and even when I did, I understood a whole new level of hell because sometimes going with what's offered feels like settling. It's a big shifting sand of attachment.

Instead, ask yourself, "What would bring me joy right now?" This question causes you to go inside where the real answers lie. They don't exist outside of you. That's what I learned from Papaji. You are already "it" so be "it" now. The only thing you have to do is get out of your own way.

"Self-love, my liege, is not so vile a sin, as self-neglecting."

-William Shakespeare, *Henry V*

"Spirituality is about walking the walk every moment."
Jill Lublin, Speaker, Strategist, Author, and Radio & TV Host

Praised as a modern day Dale Carnegie for how to be influential, Jill Lublin authored *Get Noticed...Get Referrals* and is the coauthor of the national bestselling books, *Networking Magic* and *Guerrilla Publicity*. She is the founder of GoodNews Media, Inc. and hosts the television program, *Messages of Hope*, and the nationally syndicated radio show, *Do the Dream*. Jill is a popular international speaker who teaches powerful publicity, networking, and influence strategies. She offers these techniques in her training program, which includes two CDs, three DVDs, a workbook, and card deck. Jill trains companies in innovative strategies to improve the bottom line as chief executive officer of Promising Promotion, her strategic consulting firm. Over the past twenty years, she has worked with ABC, NBC, CBS, and other national media outlets, and knows what they want. Jill has been featured in *The New York Times, Women's Day, Fortune Small Business, Entrepreneur Magazine,* and *Inc.* She also has appeared on ABC and NBC radio and national television affiliates.

Q. What experiences put you on your spiritual path?
A. It was a gradual awakening. When I was twenty-four, I began seeking because I knew there was more to life, that I was part of something larger. I enrolled in personal growth seminars and became hooked. I discovered that I am an avid learner focused on being of service to the world. This motivation supports me in getting my message out from a place of love.

Q. How did these experiences change you?
A. I have a greater sense of peace and purpose in life. This realization brings both serenity and urgency. It may sound like a contradiction, but it is not. I understand my role in the world and am committed to helping as many people as I can. As a result, I remain calm, focused, and dedicated to doing the work.

Q. What has been the most challenging part of your path?
A. Integrating spirituality into daily life. When I lived in a faith community, I meditated every morning and still do at weekend retreats. However, active spirituality is not about going to workshops, it's about walking the walk every moment. I see my life as a moving meditation that infuses spirit into everything I do—my business, personal relationships, and everyone I touch. No matter how busy I am, I always make time to say a prayer of gratitude.

Q. What is your earliest memory? Why do you remember it?
A. My family was tough. I was not always recognized and appreciated for my true self. However, from a spiritual perspective, I understand that my parents did their best and I thank them for helping me become who I am today. Having to be responsible, educated, and self-reliant at an early age taught me to love myself, accept what is, and be forgiving. I do remember my father making tuna sandwiches and taking me to Belle Isle in Detroit for my eighth birthday. These acts demonstrated how much he loved me.

Q. Who are your mentors? What have you learned from them?
A. I am eternally grateful to:
• Bill Bauman, founder of *The Center for Soulful Living*, who has been a tremendous influence in my life and a blessing of healing.
• Steve, my partner, whose caring shows me every day what unconditional love is.
• T. Harv Eker, author of *The Millionaire Mind*, who gave me

the opportunity to learn from him and speak on his stage.
- Patricia McDade, founder of *Consulting Alliance*, whose *Entrepreneurial Edge* program helped me achieve breakthrough results in my business and life.
- *Lifespring*, which started me on my spiritual path.

Q. What is the greatest challenge facing society?
A. Our rising stress level as we juggle competing demands in a society with an ever-increasing pace. We are becoming overwhelmed by the needs of our careers, clients, prospects, and families. Technology only adds to this stress by creating the expectation of immediate response. That's why making our lives an action meditation is so critical to our well-being.

Q. What are your spiritual practices for connecting to your higher purpose?
A. I walk in kindness, spreading love. I meditate when I can. I always give thanks.

Q. How do you use these practices when you get out of balance?
A. I change my internal and external environment by:
- breathing in and out evenly four times,
- asking my partner Steve for a hug,
- calling a friend for support,
- cuddling my kitties,
- drinking tea and watching *Oprah*, and/or
- spending time in nature either walking or sitting on my deck.

Being in nature is so revitalizing that I spend as much time as I can there.

Q. How do you balance planning with remaining open to opportunity?
A. I plan and remain open. On the planning side, I write down my monthly revenue goal and three specific activities I will

do to achieve it. I also segment my workday into two halves. In the morning, I do business development and in the afternoon, I meet with clients. Throughout this time, I look for spiritual guidance and opportunities as they arise.

Q. If you received $100,000, how would you spend it?

A. I would give ten percent to charity and spend the rest on renovating my home and boat, investing in real estate and spiritual education, and paying off debt.

Q. If you had thirty seconds with someone in an elevator, what three things would you tell the person to do to be joyful, peaceful, and whole?

A. • Find a ritual that works for you. For example, I schedule time to be with my spiritual teacher, and others, who nourish my connection to Spirit.

• Do things that bring you joy like exercising or talking with friends. I take kitty hug breaks.

• Ask for help. Sometimes people don't ask because they think it means they are broken. They are not. I have a network of people I can call for support and they, in turn, can call me. We are all one.

Q. What books or resources have helped you the most? Why?

A. I recommend these books:
- *The Success Principles*, by Jack Canfield
- *The Power of Focus*, by Jack Canfield, Mark Victor Hansen, and Les Hewitt
- *Bradshaw on: The Family*, by John Bradshaw
- *Codependent No More*, by Melody Beattie
- *Happy for No Reason*, by Marci Shimoff

The biggest resource has been healing through Bill Bauman's work at the Center for Soulful Living.

Q. What would you like to be written on your tombstone?
A. "Many loved her and she loved all. She gave us messages of hope." Right now I'm working on a television show called *Messages of Hope*. I want to be remembered for my kindness and for making a difference in clients' lives. People approach me all the time, letting me know how my books and courses have helped them. It's my privilege to support people with getting their messages out to the world.

Q. Anything else?
A. Getting over my story was big for me. If you face a similar challenge, I suggest working with Bill Bauman at The Center for Soulful Living (www.aboutcsl.com), and going to The Entrepreneurial Edge. Your life will transform beyond your wildest dreams.

"You can't get wet from the word water."

-Alan Watts

Reprinted from The Essence of Alan Watts (1977) with the permission of Celestial Arts.

"Turn ordinary moments holy."
Rabbi Anat Moskowitz, Religion Professor, Colorado College and Rabbi, Congregation B'nai Torah

Rabbi Anat Moskowitz serves at Congregation B'nai Torah in the Denver area and works as a high school teacher at the Denver Campus for Jewish Education. She is an Adjunct Professor of Religion at Colorado College, and served as the school's first rabbi chaplain. She was senior rabbi for Temple Shalom in Colorado Springs, Colorado for five years and served as rabbi for the United States Air Force Academy for a year while the academy rabbi was deployed. Prior to moving to Colorado, she lived in Los Angeles where she was an assistant rabbi, a middle school principal, and day school rabbi. She also worked as a chaplain for Beit Teshuvah, a facility for Jews in recovery from addictions and for Nechama, a Jewish agency serving the AIDS community. Before her rabbinic journey, Rabbi Moskowitz was a third grade teacher for ten years and a Disneyland foreign language tour guide. She received her bachelor's degree in psychology from California State University Long Beach and her master's degrees in Hebrew letters and rabbinic studies, California teacher credentials, and rabbinic ordination from the University of Judaism. She volunteers as a prison chaplain.

Q. What experiences put you on your spiritual path?
A. At age five, I was attending services with my father and said, "When I grow up, I want to be a rabbi." My father replied, "You cannot because you are a girl." So I said, "Then, I'll grow up to be a boy." My father retorted, "That's not possible." Finally, I compromised, "Then, I'll be a rabbi's wife." I knew I wanted to do something in religion and saw no separation between faith and learning. For example, I used to hold services for my friends, most of whom were Christian, where

I taught them how to read and write and pray to God. My relationship with God strengthened as I felt him embracing and comforting me after I was molested.

Q. How did these experiences change you?
A. These experiences grounded me in who I was. Since I couldn't be a rabbi, I decided to help children through becoming a psychiatrist or psychologist. By age twelve, I subscribed to *Psychology Today* and supported children's causes such as The Jerry Lewis MDA Telethon. After earning my master's degree, I grew tired of studying and became a third grade teacher. One day, a seven-year-old student named Amanda said, "You've been teaching for a while now. What are you planning to do with the rest of your life? You should become a rabbi." I replied, "But I wouldn't finish rabbinical school until age forty." Amanda countered, "You'll be forty anyway so why not be forty and a rabbi?"

I initially started the rabbinical program without really applying or even wanting to go. The school kept calling and asking when I was coming. As soon as I walked into the University of Judaism, I knew I belonged. During my first internship, I worked at Nechama, a hospital for Jewish AIDS patients. I was the "chick rabbi" who studied Talmud and Mishna with the patients and tried to reconcile their families. The internship helped me get over my fear of hospitals and death.

Q. What changes are you noticing about your life and the world?
A. During my second internship, I worked at Beit T'shuvah with recovering addicts. The clients wouldn't open up to me until I admitted my own addictions. I claimed not to have any, then finally confessed, "I'm addicted to victimhood. I use it as an excuse for not succeeding all the way and for letting people hurt me. If people treat me nicely, I push them away." From my clients, I learned that being vulnerable makes me more approachable and teaches that it's okay to stumble on your path and question God. For example, my cancer journey has

been more positive than negative, but I still get angry with God. If I hadn't taken an honest look at myself, I wouldn't be able to help others.

Q. What changes are others noticing about you?
A. Before these experiences, I was shut down. People had to work through layers to reach me. Despite having gone through cancer—and my savings along with it—I'm happier than ever. People say I'm more present and real, with a radiant smile that reaches up to my eyes. My husband is a gift from God. Our five-year marriage centers me and gives me greater perspective.

Q. What has been the most challenging part of your path?
A. My learning disability, dyslexia, has been the most challenging. I process information differently and have trouble communicating it back the way teachers want. Since I grew up with it before children were tested, I adapted by working three times harder, a good thing in a Jewish family with high educational standards. Ironically, this is one area where I never used victimhood as an excuse. Although I was put on academic probation my first year of rabbinical school, I never gave up. My professors, knowing how hard I worked, encouraged me to continue.

Q. What is your earliest memory? Why do you remember it?
A. When I was 1 ½ years old, we lived in Israel. I remember looking out the window and eating ice cream—really strawberries, bananas, sugar, and sour cream mixed together—while sitting at the table my grandfather had made me. I remember this sweet moment because I had my mom's love and attention all to myself. At age two, I recall leaving Israel and flying to the U.S. When I looked out the airplane window, I thought the clouds were house rooftops. I remarked, "Things will be different here."

Q. Who are your mentors? What have you learned from them?

A. Amanda, the student I mentioned earlier who now is in law school (my former pupils are about thirty years old). Two years into rabbinical school, I came home frustrated, threw down my holy books, and decided to drop out. I ordered a non-kosher pizza for delivery and zoned out watching Friends. The phone rang. It was Amanda. She said, "We studied Jacob's ladder today and I was thinking about how you are going to be the ladder helping people reach heaven when they are low and come back down again when they need grounding." Needless to say, I stayed in rabbinical school. Ruti Gavish, the school principal who said, "You're a wild weed and I'm going to make you a tame flower." She pushed me hard to be the best teacher I could be because she wanted to ensure I did what was right for the children. Rabbi Bradley Shavit Artson, a rabbi at the synagogue where I taught day school, who knew I'd be a rabbi ten years before I did. He had a way of explaining things that made me feel I already knew them. He assured me that the rabbinate needed me and my intuitive skills. Everyone I encounter is my mentor, like the homeless man who said, "Have a nice day," even though I did not make eye contact. What's the point of being blessed if we are not a blessing in return?"

Q. What is the greatest challenge facing society?
A. Our hyper-individuality—our myopic focus on our own needs to the detriment of society. It's like we hear only the first part of the airline safety instruction, "Put your oxygen mask on first..." and ignore "...before assisting others." I thought about this while exercising at the gym, surrounded by people plugged into their iPods and absorbed in their own worlds. However, we'd come to the gym rather than work out at home. So the sense of community is there somewhere, just as it is when natural disasters, like the tsunami, bring us together. Our challenge is to carry this sense of community into everyday life and extend ourselves beyond our own needs. When we really understand we are all in the same boat, then divisions—and the wars they bring—will fade.

Q. What advice would you give someone just starting his or her spiritual path?

A. First, grow quiet to discover who you are. Buddhist meditation offers a safe way to do this without conflicting with other religions. Second, explore the universal themes in all religions to create a patchwork that resonates. Third, use this patchwork as a starting point to find a religion that is meaningful to you. Don't rush. The word "religion" comes from "ligament," meaning "to connect." It takes time to find a community that expresses who you are.

Q. What are your spiritual practices for connecting to your higher purpose?

A. Action is my practice. I pray, serve my community, and follow Jewish customs.

• Prayer: In Latin, prayer means to beg. In Hebrew, it means to self-reflect. I meditate on a Jewish word or prayer, Shema, until I reach self-reflection. Then, I stay there.

• Community: I'm involved in the Jewish community, learning the Book of Daniel with a group of Jewish women, reading the Talmud with my study partner, and giving my husband the Jewish perspective on various topics like angels. He, in turn, tries to teach me economics, but my eyes glaze over.

• Custom: I keep kosher. Eating is a religious act; I'm careful to make all my interactions holy.

Q. How do you use these practices when you get out of balance?

A. Buddhist meditation taught me it's okay to feel my emotions and just be. Sometimes that's all it takes. Other times I'll go for a walk and look at the mountains or photos of my children to remind me of the big picture. If all else fails, I'll treat myself to chocolate, the spa, a nap, or Nordstrom's. I live for the day, finding joy in the simple pleasures. Even as a girl, I lifted my spirits at bedtime by opening the window, tasting the fresh air, and gazing at the stars. This approach to life sums up who I am.

Q. How do you balance planning with remaining open to opportunity?

A. Jews have a saying, "Man plans and God laughs." For example, cancer changed my plans for a year—so much so that it was questionable whether I'd feel well enough to attend my stepdaughter's wedding. Fortunately, I did. Whatever happens, I believe it's my life purpose to make each moment holy. The concept of making the mundane holy is central to Judaism. It's why we have blessings for everything—the mountains, the rain, and so on. So I plan my time, but when God throws a better opportunity, I take it.

Q. If you received $100,000, how would you spend it?

A. There is so much to do that $100 million would be better. First, I would support the physical, emotional, and educational needs of children exposed to violence, whether in gangs or Iraq. By support, I mean actually doing the work myself. If we do not help our children, we will have no future. I'd start there and work out to their parents, communities, and environments.

Q. If you had thirty seconds with someone in an elevator, what three things would you tell the person to do to be joyful, peaceful, and whole?

A. Do something for somebody else, even if you don't feel like it. Being someone's "footprints in the sand" may illuminate your path and, even if it doesn't, at least you will have done something good. A woman came to me for two years wanting to commit suicide. I told her, "If you want to die, go volunteer in Israel or Thailand." She replied, "But Rabbi, that's dangerous!" So I challenged her. "You don't really want to die. Go do something outside yourself." The oys and joys of life are not always about us.

Q. What books or resources have helped you the most? Why?
A. I'm a voracious reader and enjoy a wide variety of books, including:
* *When Bad Things Happen to Good People*, by Harold S. Kushner
* *Man's Search for Meaning*, by Viktor E. Frankl
* *God in Search of Man*, by Abraham Joshua Heschel
* *The Celestine Prophecy*, by James Redfield

I also like children's books such as:
* *Harold and the Purple Crayon*, by Crockett Johnson. Harold creates whatever he needs with a simple crayon.
* *Old Turtle*, by Douglas Wood and Cheng-Khee Chee. Old Turtle shows the other animals and weather elements that God created them all as equals.

My greatest resources are being in a good relationship with my husband, exercising in nature, and turning ordinary moments holy. As Heschel's book, *The Sabbath*, suggests, the Sabbath's cathedral is in time, not a physical edifice.

Q. What would you like to be written on your tombstone?
A. As in Linda Ellis' poem, *The Dash*, "Her life was so much more than the dash. She did her work with joy and found happiness in everything." I tell people to go out and do something to make God smile, to make the space you are in holy. It's like the saying, "Pray as if everything depends on God but act as if everything depends on you."

Q. Anything else?
A. My father was part of the Golda Meir group called Halutizim, founders of Israel and Kibbutz Sasa. Although my father described himself as an atheist, he handed down Jewish history and tradition to my brother and me. For example, we had to be home every Friday night for Shabbat dinner and Jewish holidays, even when we were part of our school's football game half-time show. Interestingly, when my brother al-

most died as a child, my father dropped to his knees saying, "Please God, don't let my son die!" When it mattered, he believed. My mother, on the other hand, encompassed religion in all that she did. I am a mix of my two parents.

RELIGION PROFESSOR AND RABBI

"Embrace compassion and life's ambiguity."
Eric Moya, Esalen and The Upledger Institute

Eric Moya is a Licensed Mental Health Counselor, a diplomate certified CranioSacral therapist and instructor, and founder of The Ripple Effect: Center for Mind and Body Therapy in Albuquerque, New Mexico. Eric teaches and lectures internationally on CranioSacral Therapy, lymph drainage, and health care ethics. Currently, he serves as Dean of Integral Education at the Esalen Institute in Big Sur, California. Eric has a master's degree in mental health counseling and a bachelor's degree in English literature and creative writing from the University of Houston, where he graduated magna cum laude. He also has training in neuromuscular therapy, positional release therapy, visceral manipulation and massage.

Q. What experiences put you on your spiritual path?
A. In my early twenties, I was fired from a teaching position at an elite preparatory school. My firing challenged me to take an honest look at myself and undertake significant growth. During this process, I let go of my original career plan and came to appreciate, even embrace, life's ambiguity. I learned to appreciate ambiguity even more while giving a demonstration on energy work during my CranioSacral Therapy teaching apprenticeship. I was uncomfortable with energy work and was bluffing my way through as I treated a woman with severe frozen shoulder syndrome. Her increase in range of motion was so remarkable that it would have been hard to explain scientifically. This cosmic kick in the behind helped me connect to something greater than myself and trust that it would take me where I needed to go.

Q. How did these experiences change you?
A. Before, when I focused on self and being in control, I experienced fear, desperation, and clinging. As I embraced ambiguity, I saw life from a broader perspective. Now I seek situations where I can help others appreciate ambiguity and connect with something greater. For example, when teaching CranioSacral Therapy, I model being a calm, playful therapist to help students work through frustration and trust the process. At Esalen, I create educational programs and ethical policies that foster a more mindful organization focused on helping people—and the world—self-actualize.

Q. What has been the most challenging part of your path?
A. I'm working to understand the interplay between selflessness and selfishness. I want to be as selfless as possible so as not to harm others. However, I invest so much energy in selflessness that I have not experienced selfishness in a satisfactory way. I don't want to feel guilty about having human needs. To better understand this interplay, I view selflessness as making decisions toward community, and selfishness as making decisions away from it. I define community as working together to cherish life, promote fairness, and respect different paradigms. I know a counselor who embodies this interplay with tremendous grace. I asked her how she deals with the frustrations of working with people with addictions. She replied, "I speak to the person's higher self while facing the reality right in front of us." This approach gives her such compassion despite the crumminess of humanity. She is a great role model.

Q. What changes are you noticing about your life and the world?
A. Instead of getting swept up in drama, I look at situations with a sense of perspective and humor. From this vantage point, I appreciate people's different opinions, love them where they are, and collaborate to create mutually beneficial change. This approach takes the edge off people's frustration and discord.

Q. What changes are others noticing about you?
A. Friends say I'm less anxious, uptight, and controlling. They see me as more content and accessible, openly sharing my concerns, receiving support, and giving support in turn.

Q. What is your earliest memory? Why do you remember it?
A. I remember being a baby and having my sisters prop me up with pillows so I could sit up and watch them entertain me. They enjoyed putting on plays and trying to make me laugh. I recall this memory because I loved being the center of attention. It felt good.

Q. Who are your mentors? What have you learned from them?
A. My greatest mentor is the addiction counselor I referred to earlier. She is a gifted therapist, both highly intelligent and compassionate. She's also very human, accepting others' faults, as well as her own. This compassionate realism sets her apart from other mentors and counselors. She also helped me grow as a teacher and therapist by reframing situations to knock me out of myself and get me to see from a broader perspective.

Q. What is the biggest challenge facing society?
A. We are hardwired for self-interest, making it challenging to take the path of greater good. There are individuals who have achieved selflessness but I'm not sure it is possible right now for society as a whole to attain it. For example, I want to support the free market but given our myriad self-interests—nations, races, classes, and religions—we often use power and privilege to hurt rather than help. So, for now, I focus on being good to people and seeing the effects ripple out from there.

Q. What advice would you give someone just starting his or her spiritual path?
A. Do whatever it takes to be compassionate to others and yourself. Compassion enables people to be good to each other

during conflict and forges solutions that are productive for the community. Humor also helps. Don't take situations or yourself too seriously.

Q. What are your practices for connecting to your higher purpose?

A. My practices include cultivating new perceptions and experiences, an appreciation and love for others, and a sense of wonder about the world. These practices feed a larger one of finding place and purpose in the universe. As an ethicist, part of my purpose is to create educational programs and health care practices that reflect higher moral principles.

Q. How do you use these practices when you get out of balance?

A. I remove myself from the situation so I can introspect and recover. Introspection involves understanding the other person's perspective, and my own, to return with compassion and resolve for working through it together. Ironically, boxing—an extreme example of what happens in life—has taught me a great deal about conflict management. It has given me the ability to remain calm amidst chaos and drama.

Q. How do you balance planning with remaining open to opportunity?

A. I err on the side of planning but I'm open to exploring alternatives. For example, I never planned on leaving New Mexico, where I owned a business and home. However, when the opportunity arose at Esalen, my family and I embraced it, even though it was a complete departure from our original trajectory.

Q. If you received $100,000, how would you spend it?

A. Having just moved to California, I would use it for selfish purposes so we would not live paycheck to paycheck. For example, I would set aside money for my daughter's education, as well as my own continuing studies. With fewer struggles,

I can be a better agent of what I'm already doing—creating mindful, conscious programs that help make the world a better place.

Q. If you had thirty seconds with someone in an elevator, what three things would you tell the person to do to be joyful, peaceful, and whole?
A. Seek out new experiences to cultivate compassion, happiness, and service. When you find ways to be of service, relish those moments with gusto. Being good to others serves both them and you. When they shine, you shine. Conversely, giving from a place of lack serves no one because it fosters resentment.

Q. What books or resources have helped you the most? Why?
A. I have learned a lot from existentialist psychology, which draws upon Jungian myths and archetypes. I'm a hopeful existentialist who believes that even though we don't have certainty or truth, we can create it on our own. Living my purpose to create a meaningful, actualized life is worth every penny. Photography is another great resource. When I carry my camera, I am forced to slow down, pay attention, and capture life's splendor. I also appreciate music, especially classical, which puts me in tune with my emotions. Finally, I embrace those sublime moments of grace, which come from engaging in the world's beauty.

Q. What would you like to be written on your tombstone?
A. "He was a flawed human being who loved and helped people." I tear up when I say this because I yearn to feel compassion, to embrace our humanness in both its flaws and beauties. I used to spend a lot of time cultivating the experience of shadow but it's not as much a part of my spiritual process anymore.

Q. Anything else?
A. When I first became a CranioSacral therapist and instructor,

I tried to fit everything into this paradigm and it didn't work. Humanity is too big for one paradigm. Having this realization was both a selfish and selfless act. Selfishly, I knew the lens of CranioSacral Therapy was too narrow to fit my world experience. Selflessly, seeing the world from many paradigms frees me to better serve humanity.

"Path is what's inside you. What you were born to do."
Mike Parker, Poet, Painter, Musician, and Mountaineer

Mike Parker is a poet whose published works include *Don't Fall off the Mountain, Wallflower Sutra* (book and audio CD) and *Mike Parker Live* (audio CD). His poetry is published by D'Spare Press in Boulder, Colorado, and edited by lifelong friend Phil Dubitsky. Mike has also recorded two music albums, *Total Access* and *Wet Moments* and appeared in two films, *Crossover Dreams* and *AC-DC*. In his spare time, he is a painter and mountain climber who has scaled peaks such as Mount Audubon, Sawtooth Mountain, and St. Mary's Glacier. In 1979, he was the Artist in Residence in Ward, Colorado, where he held the nation's first weeklong poetry and kickboxing event. Currently, he lives in Ward with his wife and daughter at an altitude of 9,250 feet.

Q. What experiences put you on your spiritual path?
A. My spiritual path has been poetry and painting. I write and paint about the mountains and people. I don't particularly describe it as a spiritual path because "path" becomes a thing unto itself. For much of my career, my poems have been edgy. My earlier book, *Don't Fall Off The Mountain*, is much edgier than my current one, *Wallflower Sutra*. I think paths have edges to them. It's one of the things that makes them paths. They are a way of going somewhere else. Edgy is okay with me and sometimes fun. My life has changed a lot. I'm sixty-five years old, married, and have a four-year-old daughter. So my path has been a long one, which has led to a place that is unpredictable. Four-year-olds are good at teaching you about the edges of your path.

Q. How did these experiences change you?
A. I was a conscientious objector during the Vietnam War. That

was a big step on my path because that war was the most unspiritual thing happening on the planet, as most wars are. So being in opposition was a strong chemical in my mix. It involved commitment, just like being a poet. And I was in good company, as Muhammad Ali was perhaps the best known conscientious objector.

It is a different time now, but some of the same horrible things are happening. We're still involved in a couple of wars and it still demands commitment against that way of life.

Q. What changes are you noticing about your life and the world?
A. Being in New York City in the 1980s was an edgy time. I was in the music and movie business doing all kinds of things and being fairly successful at my craft. Twenty years later, I am in Ward, Colorado, which is not New York City. Culture always changes us. Now I'm much more nature based. I still have my cultural edges, I hope, but firewood has become my medium for surviving at 9,200 feet. Keeping my family warm and fed either is a form of art or drudgery. These days it's my art form, although I still write and paint. I have a nice little studio at the end of our house where I just finished a painting. I share the space with my wife, Mary, who is a writer. So my emphasis has changed, my politics have changed.

I think things are more hopeful now, although being involved in two wars is not the most hopeful reality. But we have someone in office that is not at ease with committing murder. There is no other way to describe it when innocent people get killed for dubious reasons such as economic resources, cultural discrimination, or preserving our lifestyle. We think that the people we attack matter less than we do. I would love to see that stop. There is plenty of work to do right here at home. Detroit is the Third World. There is a massive amount of unemployment. People deserve better than that, especially when there is money to spend on war. It's crazy.

Q. What changes are others noticing about you?

A. I'm probably less relaxed. It was easy being single and climbing mountains four days a week and doing whatever I wanted to earn a living. It's more overwhelming to support a family, be a decent human being, and also produce some art. I'm a little edgier and more wrapped up in the machinery it takes to do all that. My job is a major part of my life now. For a long time, it was the least. I have a great job at the Nature's Own store. I like working with the store's minerals and fossils and dealing with people all day long. It is a very theatrical job with a language and culture of its own. As a performer, I always know when I am on stage and at work, I am definitely on stage. So it's important to use this theater to affect my art in a positive way. My venues may have changed but it is still incredibly important to be on the edge, communicating with people from that place. You either use it or lose it. I try to rationalize forty hours a week away from home and painting and writing this way.

Q. What has been the most challenging part of your path?

A. Earning a living. In any society, there is room at the top for only so many people. For poets, this is not an easy part of the path and that is where commitment comes in. The most likely way out is to become a university professor. I have done some teaching, but that part of the path never appealed to me. It did not produce the kind of art I was looking for. The culture of New York City in the 1980s was much more of a university than any college in the United States. It was a real breeding ground for great artists such as Keith Haring and Jean-Michel Basquiat. They are now dead and their paintings sell for millions.

Having a family and earning a living as an artist requires even more commitment. My daughter Frankie is as important as any damn poem in the world. And working at the store pays the bills much better than poetry. Landlords are never fond of taking poems instead of money. I still paint and write, but it takes me longer to produce work now that I have more on my plate. My wife is here all day so her job is much harder than mine and requires greater commitment. I, at least, get to go out into the world and then come home. This is my path now and it's different from being a punk rocker in New York City playing in front of 5,000 people and going out in the street the next day and having everybody say, "How are you doing? That was a great show!" This way my fame comes with a little kid and diapers. I'm a lucky guy to have run into Mary and to have Frankie between us. And I love living in this great little town. We are all connected to nature so that part of our path is very solid.

Q. What is your earliest memory? Why do you remember it?
A. I remember being an opinionated kid who liked being in motion and doing what he wanted to do. I grew up in a blue-collar factory culture. My dad worked hard but we were poor. From the beginning, motion has been a major ingredient because it is important to my sense of self, or non-self. I am here. Realizing this is essential because we try to forget two things all day long: the incredible experience of being born and then dying. These are the most uncommon, most un-mundane things you could imagine. And we try to forget them most of the day and go on like neither one has, or ever will, happen. Being in motion is part of being alive.

Q. Who are your mentors? What have you learned from them?
A. My politics were emerging when I went to the University of New Haven during the Vietnam War. There I met a guy named Bertrand Mathieu, a poet who took me in as a friend and allowed me to develop my skills as a performer. Bert turned me on to a lot of writers, which resulted in publishing some of my first poems with Anaïs Nin and appearing in early magazines with Allen Ginsberg. Through this exposure, I got to know the whole beat world and did some performances with them. That culture had an incredible effect on me.

When I left college, I moved to Manhattan's Lower East Side, became a conscientious objector, and got my first job at Brentano's bookstore. I worked there with Robert Mapplethorpe, whose roommate was the poet Patti Smith. They were some of my very first friends in New York. We were all committed to a life of art and we all got our wish. I just read Patti's new book. She's a wonderful artist. And Robert became the most famous photographer ever. They were really interesting, really nice people. Commitment was a huge thing to us and we were committed to death. Even if we did not have anything going on, we were committed. We were on this path. That's what path takes. It's like climbing a mountain. Getting to the top is a long process—overcoming obstacles and different environments. You have to adjust your breathing, your will, and everything else to get where you are going. I think all paths entail these things. I like to climb these mountains [gesturing to the Indian Peaks in Colorado]. They are wonderful places.

Q. What is the greatest challenge facing society?
A. Replacing outdated cultural models that destroy the environment, our capability to love, and the value of people's labor. These models take the joy out of life. In a lot of ways, it is compassion versus violence. We have to change our approach because it is leading down some paths that have no return. The path may disappear behind us and we will have nowhere to go. That certainly has happened in our relationship with nature. We have extracted things, burned them, and poisoned the elements. We need to learn how to fit into the scheme of the natural world without being the dominant factor. Up here in the mountains, we are a little more aware of this because in February, we are not the dominant factor. Only behind the closed doors of our homes are we the dominant factor and there we have to burn a lot of wood to maintain this status. That's because the weather outside is much bigger than we are. It's the same when I go on a snowshoe trip up towards the divide. I have to fit in and not be

the dominant factor. And that's a good feeling. It has been a male dominated culture for a long time, which has led to some places that are hard to get out of.

Q. What advice would you give someone just starting his or her spiritual path?

A. The only reason to pick a path akin to mine is because it is not even really a choice. It's what is inside you, what you were born to do. And people have many different ways of going about it. If it is your path, make a commitment to it outside of success or fame. Just do it because it is what you love. And if you love it, you'll be good at it. And doing it is the only way to get good at it. In the music business, you're never totally free because you are involved in an industry. Being a solitary poet or painter is just as hard, but for different reasons, mainly financial ones. There is nothing wrong with being famous enough to pay the rent and take care of your needs. But whether that is something that happens all the time or only once in a while, you still have to stay on your path. Commitment is everything.

I have known a lot people who got famous and most of them are pretty nice. They are very committed artists. But there is only so much room for a particular niche and there are millions of others who scratch in a notebook at night and nobody is ever going to hear them. But they feed the culture. They make art possible. They are just as major a component as those who are well known and have an easier time making a living.

Q. What are your practices for connecting to your higher purpose?

A. I would love to tell you that I sit down and do Zen meditation twice a day but this is no longer the case. My day has become my path as I support my family and try to be a good dad and husband. I hitchhike to work every morning and that's a time when I can breathe, clear my mind, and become aware of myself. At work, my practice is how I treat and relate to people. My daughter has a way of sweeping my path for me whether I like it or not. Her reality is startlingly clear, right there in front of me as she puts her arms around me. I'm all for being able to sit a couple of times a day and create a little peaceful space. But I don't always have time for that. And when I do, it is standing by the road hitchhiking. When you are hitchhiking, you can't force the ride. So sometimes being still and waiting is a major part of it. Otherwise it is drudgery, especially in bizarre weather on a February morning. You get your face washed in a different way. Sometimes, I am not the most important person on my path. I think that is a big lesson for me at this point in my life.

Q. How do you use these practices when you get out of balance?

A. Sometimes I am a schmuck like everybody else. I just am, even when I don't mean to be. We all have engrained attitudes that reemerge in us, which are self-centered and easy to fall into. I feel bad when I am like that, especially with Mary and Frankie. They both are very forgiving. I am fortunate to share a path with them. I have a lot to learn.

Q. How do you balance planning with remaining open to opportunity?

A. I have to be more open than planned because I hitchhike to work. At the store, I have some regular tasks, but I always remain open to whoever walks in the door and that's the theatrical element. It is very much a stage and an opportunity to relate to who and what is right in front of me. I sell more of my books at the store than anywhere else in the world. I watch a lot of people buy them who don't have the slightest idea they are mine. Sometimes I sell paintings there too. And it's great when somebody says, "Oh, I love that painting up there. How much is it?" When I finally mention it's mine, it's a lot of fun.

My job is a lot like being a bartender because I don't have any control over who comes in and what their mood is. Some days I meet extraordinarily knowledgeable people. People come to the store because they have a geological background and love fossils and rocks. Others come because they are seeking minerals for spiritual reasons. So I just try and stay open to my day. And then I come home and have to be open to another kind of day.

Q. If you received $100,000, how would you spend it?

A. I would say, "Give me the $100,000 right now and I'll show you." Just kidding. It's really a tough question because, in my heart, I am an old-fashioned pinko commie. I know communism did not turn out to be the most ideal system but I'd still like to share my fortune with everybody. I would also like to buy a little house for my family. But my wife would be the first to advise giving the funds away to a friend in need. She's right. We always manage to have a roof over our heads and good food to eat. That's all we really need.

I think money is fun and it should be even more fun for people. Right now, it is too hard to get. This economy has taught us about greed. Money is no guarantee of happiness. Even when we are broke, if we have love, then it is worth so much more. I'm not looking to make a lot of money. I'm looking to take care of my family. It's great to do a poetry reading, or show a painting, and get paid for my craft. But that's not why I'm an artist. I earn my money by going to work every day. And it's not a bad thing. It has a certain freedom to it.

Q. If you had thirty seconds with someone in an elevator, what three things would you tell the person to do to be joyful, peaceful, and whole?

A. When the elevator stops, get off and go where you are going with purpose.

Q. What books or resources have helped you the most? Why?

A. Books. I read a lot of books. Being influenced by other artists can only help you on your path. Indulge yourself as deeply as possible in works from all over the world. My favorite poet is Gary Snyder. I like many different kinds of poetry but to me, Gary's books are friends. They are as warm and meaningful as my human friends. The vision of his work has fed and sustained me through both difficult and wonderful times. If you are going to be an artist, it is important to stay open to every kind of work. When I was a kid in New York, I would go out five nights a week and listen to every type of music. This fed who I was on stage. Being open is an essential element to your growth as an artist and person. Stop your mind gossip long enough to drink it in and enjoy what's right before your eyes.

Resources. I like to take a trip once a week. Recently, I went snow shoeing up at Lake Isabel. There was still twenty feet of snow on the ground, so nobody else was up there. That feeds me. It fuels my heart and chops me down to size. I come home ready to paint and write. I get out there as much as I can. The nice thing about living in Ward is that I am out in nature. I have this rhubarb plant for a neighbor [pointing at the plant]. I just love living in the mountains.

Being nice is also important. You can be smart, successful, and good at what you do, but if you are not nice, who gives a hoot. We also need humor, the ability to laugh at ourselves. There's got to be humor; otherwise your politics or vision can back someone into a corner. Humor is what lets us out.

Q. What would you like to be written on your tombstone?
A. I'd like Mary to take my remains for a walk up one of our favorite peaks and toss me to the wind. That form of burial would be a lot of fun. I'm not sure what I think about death. I'm not even sure there is death. Stuff just tends to change form. We morph and go somewhere else, but our stuff is still our stuff. Working in the store with fossils and meteorites

reminds me of this every day. Now even thinking there is one universe seems like an antiquated idea. While our path has edges, the universe may not. It's hard to know. What we do know is that we were all born and we are all going to die. And this is a great gift.

It's not important what people say about me. That's going to be a product of how I lived my life, how I touched people, and how they touched me. Some will remember me as a total schmuck, some as a poet, and some as a father and husband. I have been many things to many people. Six months after I am gone, fewer and fewer will remember me. The world will go on. Hopefully, I will be fertilizer for something else in the universe.

Q. What do you think of the concept that my enemy is my lover?
A. I think it's great because it is really easy to be loving, kind, and compassionate towards people who like you. But to love someone who is your enemy takes a lot more work. If there is one message that the Dalai Lama has on his lips at all times, it would be that. The people who are hard to love need compassion from us, from life, from nature, from everything. The other way is really easy and, on the surface, looks more holy and enlightened. But if love has not been tested, then it does not have legs. It'll never go anywhere except in your own space. Being able to reach out, find common ground, and love things in opposition to you is what will change the world.

Q. Anything else?
A. I didn't talk about Buddhism but a lot of my sentiments are there. I think it's a wonderful path. It's a religious path without God and that always makes it interesting. I used to teach at the Boulder County Jail. If you wanted to study with Allen Ginsberg in the early days of Naropa University, you had to go to the workshop at the jail. All his students and friends, the beats, came and read there. Being at the jail was part of

my political vision. I was a judge at the time, so it was a way of balancing that out. Allen was a very political guy and he knew it was good for poets to see people on the inside and experience them as creative human beings. He also knew that poetry fed something that was different than what got people into jail in the first place. The guy was ethical, a great poet and human being, and a staunch Buddhist in his dealings with people.

When I was working at the Boulder County Jail, a kid was incarcerated for slapping Chögyam Trungpa Rinpoche, the founder of Naropa. The kid was a Buddhist who thought he had done the right thing in reaction to Trungpa Rinpoche's drinking. I spoke with Allen Ginsberg, who was influential in the Buddhist community, and said, "It's not right that this kid is in here." But Allen felt his hands were tied as the Karmapa was coming to town and there was pressure to keep the kid locked up. When the Karmapa arrived, Allen hosted a poetry reading to which over 2,000 people came. Allen said I could read anything I wanted so I read a poem called, Om, Money, Money, Money, which I had written about this kid's plight. In the poem, I compared the Karmapa to Idi Amin. Some of the crowd clapped while the rest wanted to attack me. My friend actually got up to defend me holding a clog in one hand and his son in the other. Anne Waldman, a fellow poet, leaned over and said, "That was a career limiting move." In my eyes, that was the only move. Being an artist means telling the truth, no matter how edgy. Anything, even Buddhism, can be corrupted by money, power, and fame. A Buddha doesn't need bodyguards.

"When we come into contact with the other person, our thoughts and actions should express our mind of compassion, even if that person says and does things that are not easy to accept. We practice in this way until we see clearly that our love is not contingent upon the other person apologizing or being lovable."

-Thich Nhat Hanh

Reprinted from Transformation & Healing: Sutra on the Four Establishments of Mindfulness (1990) by Thich Nhat Hanh with permission of Parallax Press, Berkeley, California. www.parallax.org.

"I am learning how to love in a healthy way, being playful and open to God."
The Rev. Diana Peters, Intercession Episcopal Church

Diana Peters is an Episcopal priest in the Diocese of Colorado. She was ordained in 1996, following seminary training at Church Divinity School of the Pacific in Berkeley, California. Before entering the priesthood, Diana was a school drama teacher and a marketing manager in the automated mapping industry. She has been married to her husband Gary since 1981 and has two sons, a stepdaughter, and four grandchildren. She lives in Thornton, Colorado, where she is the rector of Intercession Episcopal Church.

Q. What experiences put you on your spiritual path?
A. I have a memory, whether real or a dream, of the angels preparing me to be born. The angels said, "Remember, you have to breathe in and out, in and out." I was worried I would forget and they replied, "Don't worry. Your body is so marvelously made, it will do it for you." This experience started me on my spiritual path.

As a child, I loved going to church. I especially liked singing and communion, feeling drawn to the sacramental side of worship. As an adult, I was an active lay minister. When I finished a ministry, I'd ask God what I should do next. One time God replied, "I want you to become a priest." At first I doubted. When the desire became almost overwhelming, I followed God's will.

We think it's easy to follow God's will. After all, God said, "I will be a lantern unto your feet." But in ancient times, lanterns were tiny pots that cast only enough light to take a few steps. So it's exciting and scary to follow God's will, to see only a few steps ahead and decide to follow anyway.

Q. How did these experiences change you?
A. I've grown from them. When I had an autoimmune disease, I studied biochemistry to better understand what was happening to my body. I was amazed by how rapidly our bodies change. Our souls are even more amazing in how they grow and evolve. God placed us here to learn to be better lovers and to receive lessons that will help us. When bad things happen, God uses the experience to right our path and redeem us in love, if we allow it. When I was eight years old, I found a crown of thorns while walking through the forest during Holy Week. The crown was God's personal gift to me. I took it home and hid it so that I could keep it to myself. Later, when I tried to find it, it was gone. This lesson grew my soul. It taught me that if I have a gift, I must share it, or I may lose it.

Q. What has been the most challenging part of your path?
A. The most challenging part has been finding blessing in tragedy. Three years ago, I stopped financially supporting my son, who is an alcoholic, because it was worsening his situation. I was afraid he would be evicted and end up homeless. While counting down the days to his eviction, I had a rare heart attack called, Takotsubo Syndrome, which is nicknamed Broken Heart Syndrome.

I went to a therapist to help find the blessing in this tragedy. She said, "If we come to Earth for a purpose, what purpose is your son fulfilling in your life? What if the soul that is your son chose this life in order to help you grow. Think of the sacrifice that would be."

This discussion encouraged me to look at things differently. Yes, there has been tragedy, but also great learning. I've learned how to let go, to care for my heart, to pray for someone when I don't know how, and to keep hope when all looks hopeless. My son recently had a relapse and is homeless. So here I am again, learning how to love in a healthy way without letting it destroy him or me.

Q. What changes are you noticing about your life and the world?
A. I grew up feeling like I had to save the world. As a parent, I fixed my kids' mistakes. I don't do that now because I've learned that people do not grow if I rescue them. My autoimmune disease helped me learn this lesson too. I had to give up celebrating Holy Communion because I physically was unable to raise my hands in the *Orans* position. After six months of healing, I returned to the church and found that life had gone on as usual. This was a great lesson in letting go and allowing people to do what God called them to do.

Now I'm more hopeful about the world. We still have crises, but our global awareness and connectedness give us better ways to address them. When the Millennium Goals came out, I didn't think we could achieve them. Now I wear this braid in my hair to remind me that we are all one, with the beads representing my contributions to the goals. To deny our poverty is to deny an important piece of who we are.

Q. What changes are others noticing about you?
A. That I don't take things as personally. In the past, when people left our parish, I viewed it as a personal failure. Now I see it as God's will and, therefore, good. Maybe they have gotten what they needed from us and are ready to move on to grow their souls. I know I felt this way each time I transitioned to a new church community.

Q. What is your earliest memory? Why do you remember it?
A. When I was five years old, my mother took us to a strict church where I was required to memorize bible verses for Sunday school. I cried all the way to church because memorizing King James verses was an impossible feat. I remember praying to be the last child asked to recite so I could hear the

others and remember more. Now, working with kids, I give them nourishing experiences of God filled with joy and wonder so they won't feel fear.

Q. Who are your mentors? What have you learned from them?
A. Rev. Paul Collins (Methodist), my childhood minister who taught me about God the Father's power in creating the world and giving us rules. Sister Annacita, a Roman Catholic nun, who taught me about Jesus' love, the Holy Spirit, and miracles. The Rev. Sara Balcomb, an early female Episcopal priest, who guided me through my discernment process and encouraged me to hear God's call. The Rev. Carolyn Davis, another Episcopal priest, who helped me heal from childhood experiences and see them as assets in the priesthood. The Reverends Rick Meyers and Douglas Dunn, in whose service I learned who I am as a priest. Katherine Rowe, a layperson whose imagination and creativity inspire me. The preschool children who open my eyes to new ways of seeing God. Everyone is my mentor in some way.

Q. What is the biggest challenge facing society?
A. Our biggest challenge is unity. To realize the kingdom is to realize we are all one. Jesus prayed ". . . that they may all be one, just as you, Father, are in me, and I in you, that they also may be in us." (John 17:21) When we feel fear, we isolate ourselves, retreating inward as we erect barriers outside. We see this in the borders between Israel and Palestine and between the U.S. and Mexico. The church is experiencing this fragmentation too, because we can't agree to disagree. This breaks God's heart. We can believe different things and still be unified.

Q. What advice would you give someone just starting his or her spiritual path?
A. My advice would be to play, have fun, and remain open to surprise. I first learned the importance of play while walking a labyrinth at Grace Cathedral in San Francisco. Labyrinths

represent our life path. On the way in, we lay down our burdens. When we reach the center, we sit quietly and wait for God's message. Once received, we walk back out, integrating God's message into our lives as we pick up our duties with new perspective and levity.

When I laid down my concerns, including a dying friend, some were easy to let go, others more challenging. However, each time I laid one down, I grew lighter. When I got to the labyrinth's center, I heard God say, "Play." As I went back out and picked up each of my duties, I heard God say, "Play with it." When I started to pick up my dying friend, God said, "Leave her with me." So I left her with God at the foot of the altar, knowing she would be okay and feeling at peace. I came out of the labyrinth skipping and joyful. Maybe that's how each of us should approach our life's spiritual walk.

Q. What are your practices for connecting to your higher purpose?
A. I'm not as disciplined in spiritual practices as, say, the monastics. My conversations with God are more ongoing and impromptu, with spiritual practices changing daily. For example, I may say in the shower, "Lord, please wash me clean of my ungracious thoughts." Or I may feel a guardian angel watching over me as I drive home in the snow. I may even have a silly or mundane conversation with Jesus in the car. I'm the most disciplined during worship services, especially our Wednesday evening prayer service, in which we pray in the monastic tradition. All these practices help bring me closer to God.

Q. How do you use these practices when you get out of balance?
A. Just practicing being present with God gives me more balance. It's a source of grace. One time a parishioner was angry because he had asked me to facilitate a program, which I delegated to someone who did not follow through. The pa-

rishioner started yelling at me. Normally I would have been defensive, but I felt God's grace and extended compassion to this man. I thought of the regret he would feel later about the things he had said. My goal is to reexperience this moment of grace—to step back, gain perspective, and be that non-anxious presence for another.

Q. How do you balance planning with remaining open to opportunity?
A. As a priest, I have to be flexible. Things happen and I must respond. Uncertainty used to scare me, but I'm slowly learning to let go and let God reveal a better plan. So I make the plan, but I'm more willing to be spontaneous and allow God to surprise me with amazing solutions.

Q. If you received $100,000, how would you spend it?
A. I'd like to give some of it to the church, some of it to the organizations working toward the Millennium Goals, and some of it to my grandchildren's education. With the rest, I'd go to the Holy Land again. Only this time, I'd take my husband and a group from the church. It's a wonderful place and I'd like to share it with the people I love. Gee, I'll probably need more than $100,000!

Q. If you had thirty seconds with someone in an elevator, what three things would you tell the person to do to be joyful, peaceful, and whole?
A. Be your authentic self. Discover and embrace who God created you to be. Our maladies come from trying to be something we are not. During Holy Baptism, I ask parents and godparents to help their ". . . child to grow into the full stature of Christ." This means encouraging the child to live as Jesus did, developing fully into the person God created him or her to be. It's not easy. Our parents, teachers, friends, and the media all tell us what to be. We must ignore peer—and our own—pressure, just as Jesus did in the desert and the Garden of Gethsemane.

Q. What books or resources have helped you the most? Why?
A. The church community has been a valuable resource for growing my soul because of the support and encouragement I've receive from people. The Bible stretches my soul with difficult passages that demand my attention, even if I don't want to hear them. A gruff, old seminary professor once told me, when I complained about some of the scriptures, "It's in the Canon, deal with it." Since I also heard him say, "The Bible is a living document," I deal with it by relating the passages to my life today. *The Book of Common Prayer* helps us express our souls by weaving together scripture and prayer to unite us in our beliefs and to praise God's wonders. I often hear the best of our theology at funeral services, for example.

Q. What would you like to be written on your tombstone?
A. I am planning to be cremated, but if I had a tombstone, it would say, "Remember me as loving you." Having people know we love them is our highest calling. I borrowed this phrase from the Cowley Fathers, an Anglican community of priests who bear witness to Christ through their monastic vows and lives of service.

Q. Anything else?
A. It concerns me how many people believe there is only one way to "be saved." I've had people come to me at funerals and say they are scared for their deceased love one because she or he never accepted Jesus. I've asked, "Did the person love you? And did you love the person?" When they replied, "Yes," I reminded them that Jesus taught us that God is love. If the person was capable of loving, then God was part of them. Jesus said, "I did not lose a single one of those you gave me." (John 18:9) I'm disappointed when churches use scare tactics to get people to behave as they want.

A Roman Catholic psychotherapist, whose brother committed suicide after suffering from severe depression, came to me because she feared her brother would not go to heaven. I asked, "Was your brother's depression an illness?"

She replied, "Yes."

"If someone died of cancer, would you think he couldn't be with God?

She replied, "No."

"Then why wouldn't your brother be with God? He died from a disease just a deadly and out of his control as cancer."

Some diseases are so challenging they have to be cured in God's loving arms. I'd like us to realize God's immense compassion. We're deceiving ourselves defining God so narrowly.

"Cultivate your neutral witness. Then frequencies just pass through."
Denye Robbins, Cofounder, Journeys for Conscious Living

Denye and her husband Robert are the cofounders of Journeys for Conscious Living (J4CL), an organization that leads the world in conscious living through thoughtful changes in how we live our lives every day, thus creating the space and energy to stay centered and expand the community. J4CL hosts world class events and speakers for people to gain power. J4CL creates empowering experiences for discovering and developing a life of passion, purpose and contribution. J4CL promotes cross-cultural, universal acceptance of people, who are striving for togetherness as well as the empowerment and healing of every living being on the planet. J4CL creates opportunities, collaboration and communities for individuals and businesses to reach their full, highest potential, while experiencing love, joy and transformation.

Q. What experiences put you on your spiritual path?
A. I didn't grow up in a family that was churched. In my mid-thirties, I was given a book called *The Queen of the Cosmos*, which had a lot of Catholic doctrine in it. The book sent me into a search for the truth because I could not agree with its message. There was so much fear about what it meant to be chosen, baptized, and accepted into an organized religion. I began to read spiritual texts, attend seminars, and sit at the feet of master teachers. I visited power places on the planet and received energetic transmissions from beings that have a lot of light and wisdom. Most of the master teachers were saying the same things, but they were also saying that our way is the only way. So my search continued for absolute truth—not perspective, manipulative, or controlling truth.

I'm almost forty-eight now, so the last fifteen years have been quite a journey. I am doing what everybody is doing: gaining more awareness, growing and evolving, and becoming more tolerant and loving of others and myself. I'm moving into the core message of all the master teachers, which is that the fast path to consciousness is forgiveness—forgiveness of self, others, and God for the world being as it is. This is what the Buddha called acceptance. The Buddha's message is that all suffering stems from lack of accepting what is. I am finding that through acceptance of self, I can better accept others and give them peace.

Q. How did these experiences change you?
A. I've been doing what's called cultivating the neutral witness, that part of us that is not attached to good or bad, right or wrong, or like it or don't like it. These are called polar opposites or dualities. When I cultivate my neutral witness, or divine observer, I don't get pulled out of my core. My core is the truth of who I am instead of the spin of who I think I am.

Q. What changes are you noticing about your life and the world?
A. I don't feel responsible to fix it, teach it, or preach it. I really get now that God is on duty and I can be off. All the suffering in the world doesn't have to be mine to make better. Souls come in with lessons, challenges, and their own plans for growth and expansion. It's arrogant of me to think that I can do their work for them. True humility is being divine hands on the planet and still knowing that God is in charge. He hasn't lost their files, or mine. Everything is perfect no matter how it looks or feels. We take bodies and come down here for these dualities—good and bad, pleasure and pain, desire and fear, and like it or don't like it. In the movie *City of Angels*, an angel is weeping at our experience and people say something like, "You are bleeding, you are crying. Why? We don't like it." He replies with something like, "Life is the most beautiful thing. You can't have glorious, peaceful days without also having blood and tears."

Q. What changes are others noticing about you?
A. As a child, I grew up sensitive. I felt my stuff, my emotions, and my pain. I also felt, sensed, and internalized others' pain. This is because I understood suffering. I was the one in school who knew outcomes before they happened. Now the more I cultivate my neutral witness and stay in my core, the less I am pulled by emotions. I can still empathize with people's suffering but no longer need to merge with it and try to make it better. Instead, I can hold a space for people's empowerment and growth, knowing they have their own core, assignments, and processes to go through.

I identify a lot with the Divine Mother (the Queen of the Cosmos) and Kwan Yen, who hear the cries of the world. I hear them too. I watch movies and burst into tears or see people win and share their elation. But my job is to be compassionate and to not take it all on as my own.

Q. What has been the most challenging part of your path?
A. Knowing enough to be dangerous. Sitting in seminars and at the feet of master teachers enabled me to gather lots of data. I coach and mentor with Greg Mooers, the Quantum Monk, and we talk about beings that are in "knowing." When I am in "knowing," I am not open. I am not in listening mode waiting for the universe to guide me. So the challenging part is getting out of the teachings from the books and seminars—and what they say about the author's or seminar leader's experience—and moving into offering what I know and don't know and being okay with that. It's not feeling like the next seminar or teacher has the answer, but that inside me, in my core where there is ultimate truth, I have the answers. Nothing is missing.

Q. What is your earliest memory? Why do you remember it?
A. When I was three years old, I was in my grandmother's kitchen on Easter Sunday. She was preparing something with a French fry cooker. I was hopping through her kitchen and my hand hit the cooker and the grease went all over my body.

It's such a memory of shock, shattering, and a cosmic, Why *did this happen to my little body?* I understood that the rest of the world was celebrating the glory of God and the Resurrection and that I was in trauma and pain floating in sulfur water for three months. It's a memory that runs through my body like post-traumatic stress disorder, activating the pain in me so I can relate to the pain of others. The incident expanded my field so much that my body became a pain detector. I carry the skin grafts, the marks on my legs and hips. I don't carry them on my face. My grandmother saw what was happening and pulled on my arm so my face went in the opposite direction.

Q. Who are your mentors? What have you learned from them?
A. Many of the master teachers with whom I have studied are not on this side of the veil. I have a few that are. With delight and gratitude, I would like to mention Leslie Temple-Thurston with CoreLight. She represents the Divine Mother and she helps me in many ways, on the inner planes, in the dream plane, with untying my knots in consciousness, and with my separation issues—mainly through the original sin program and the human imprint. Steven Sadleir, with Self-Awareness Institute, has also taught me much about projecting authority, equality, love, and transmission of Shakti energy and light. I'm currently studying with Greg Mooers. He is one of the first people on the planet, with the exception of my husband Robby, that I have been able to completely trust with an open mind and heart.

On the other side of the veil, they would be Mary the Divine Mother, Kwan Yen, Christ, Buddha, and Yogananda. Yogananda represents the bridge between Eastern and Western tradition. The West, specifically America with its our Judeo-Christian tradition, has a princess archetype. We feel we are the chosen ones. I have gained so much wisdom and beauty from the Eastern faiths. Our company, Journeys for Conscious Living, is the epitome of the bridge from East to West in helping balance the energies of the world through instituting teachings from both sides of the planet. Yogananda has been showing up for me in different ways. I found out early on at the House of the Mother in Santa Fe, New Mexico, that Leslie has lineage with Yogananda. Recently, Greg said he studied with him. There is this connection with Yogananda in my soul pod.

Q. What is the greatest challenge facing society?
A. The balancing of masculine and feminine energies. We've had two thousand years of patriarchal rule and, before that, matriarchal rule. Now we have reached a point where humanity has a chance of creating real equality between the masculine and feminine. Remember when men owned women, children, and animals? They were listed as possessions in the property of deeds. Things have changed. We are beginning to understand the value of every sentient being—what animals, children, teenagers, women, and the elderly bring. There is a huge shift happening on the planet and people are just walking into it. All is equal in the quantum field. Heaven and Earth are one in the same. What we focus on is what we will create. For the first time there is such hope that we will create this balance.

Q. What advice would you give someone just starting his or her spiritual path?
A. Everyone is on the path whether he or she knows it or not. There is no starting or stopping. You are on it. That future God pull is in each of us. So who's doing the work exponentially? Who's saying, "I get that these are conditioned patterns I'm playing out and I'm willing to navigate my way through consciousness a little quicker." Dr. David Hawkins says that twelve to fifteen percent of the planet is actually signing up for this exponential expansion. Why? Because the old paradigm is dying out. People are moving away from playing tyrant and victim and into living from their hearts. It's exciting to peek over the fence at this new heart-centered paradigm.

Q. What are your practices for connecting to your higher purpose?

A. Cultivating my neutral witness. During meditation I ask myself, "How aware, conscious, and grounded am I today?" Skip Lackey, who does The Journey work, gave me this album with a song called "Praises for the World," by Jennifer Berezan. I start and end the day listening to it. It's about getting into that space of gratitude for all the beautiful things and challenges and everything else that shows up to help my soul accumulate wisdom.

Also helpful is not being attached to outcome. For me, there is always somewhere to go. So Greg will say to me, "Den, where do you think 'there' is?" I'll say, "I don't know." Then he'll ask, "Where are you standing right now?" I'll say, "Here." He'll reply, "Okay, go over there. Where are you standing now?" I'll say, "Here." And he'll reply, "Oh, so you're 'here.' Then, 'there' is not there, only here." What a great lesson to know that I am here and now. Where else is there to go? I'm already home. Like Dorothy in *The Wizard of Oz*, I never really left to begin with. So I'm always looking down at my invisible ruby slippers saying, "There's no place like home, there's no place like home, there's no place like home."

Q. How do you use these practices when you get out of balance?

A. When I notice that I've lost my neutral witness, I check in and say, "What's this about, a past trauma or parental program?" Since I'm an empath, I might also say, "Is this my stuff or someone else's?" Before my spiritual search, I would spin for days, weeks, and months over other people's stuff or my own. Now it takes me five or ten minutes to notice what's up and unhook from my reaction or emotion. Instead of beating myself up, I say, "This madness, frustration, or elation is not me, it is just passing through." Then I go back to my core because that is who I really am.

I also surround myself with people who remind me when I am not in my core. I have given them permission to say, "Den, you are out of your center. I invite you to look at where you are projecting, liking or disliking, or getting stuck in a conditioned pattern." So having playmates or helpers in the garden is a great source of support. Oprah says, "My secretary is smarter than I am. I like it that way. I surround myself with people who are smarter because they help me fly." It's like the slipstream thing geese do. We all know when it's our turn to be at the head of the V-formation and when it's our turn to fly behind and let someone else help us out.

Q. How do you balance planning with remaining open to opportunity?

A. I'm the mother of five who has children, a community, a partner, and business colleagues relying on me. So there has to be a certain amount of planning. What I do is give the universe my order. I offer it up saying, "In Denye's world, this is how I have planned my day." Then I leave room for magic. I understand that my agenda may not have the big picture so I am open to the divine sending this or something better. Or taking a lesson, learning from it, and letting it go. I show up every day and do the best I can while leaving room for magic.

Q. If you received $100,000, how would you spend it?

A. I would spend it on things that further the mission of Journeys for Conscious Living. Our team has decided that we are going to be a platform for master teachers to deliver their visions and messages to the world. Robby and I have done so much seminar work that we are able to hold a space for others who want transformation, expansion, and enlightenment. We provide this safe, soft place where people can get out of their comfort zones and have experiences that pull them toward their dharma or purpose without judgment, limits, conditioning, or fears. And they get to do the work with like-minded people who show up and say, "We're up for it! We want to take a look at the new paradigm too."

Q. If you had thirty seconds with someone in an elevator, what three things would you tell the person to do to be joyful, peaceful, and whole?

A. I would remind them that they are not their good or bad days, or their dark or light side, but that they are all of it, all the time. And that this, too, shall pass. You can never be anything other than who you already are—and that is whole, perfect, complete, and precious. You are a contributor and a hero, a divine child of God who has the right to show up in this elevator feeling a little bit down today. It's okay to be where you are and not have to fix it or make it better. Just be with your experience because maybe that's the thing that is going to allow you to have more joy.

Q. What books or resources have helped you the most? Why?

A. What supports me is aligning myself with things that are life affirming, that vibrate at a high frequency of consciousness. This goes back to Dr. David Hawkins' work with the map of consciousness. We can use these calibrated levels of consciousness as a discernment tool. For example, I prefer to spend time with people who are doing consciousness work. They remind me who I am when I forget and they depend on me to do the same for them. I also prefer to eat foods filled with life force and to take antioxidants and marine phytoplanktons that repair my cells and build the new spiritual DNA. Being optimum in our bodies supports our mental, emotional, and spiritual well-being. They are all connected.

Water is another resource. We have a container of it upstairs with the words "love, harmony, and balance" written underneath, much like Dr. Masaru Emoto's work as seen in the film *What the Bleep!?* When I am in the bathtub, I like to submerge myself, going all the way under into that amniotic, pre-cave experience of the womb. Sometimes I add a few drops of essential oils to help lift my vibration.

I also do sound and toning work with a woman named Aurelia who plays the Tibetan singing bowls, the didgeridoo, and crystal bowls and teaches about the healing properties of sound.

I like spending time with the very young and old. Kids have no agenda, so I enjoy watching their freedom, authenticity, and joy. I also relish sitting at the feet of someone who has been on the planet longer than I have. There is nothing better than having a group of older women around saying, "I've got a thing or two to tell you about womanhood, yourself, and all the little children that we have birthed, nurtured, and supported. That crone wisdom is one of my favorite things. The book *The Secret Life of Bees* speaks to that with its Black Madonna and other archetypes. It's hands down the best book for me.

Other things that amplify my vibration include saying prayers, listening to inspirational music, watching birds, having crystals and enlightened rocks in my home, and getting outdoors and connecting to the Earth grid. I am lucky. I have been blessed with the resources to do and see a lot.

Q. What would you like to be written on your tombstone?
A. I would like to be remembered as a person who empowered others, who helped them understand that they are way more than they think they are. I'd also like to dispel the lie that we are poor, pitiful sinners begging our way back into heaven's gate. We have never been anything other than held in love, grace, and perfection. Even when things look the darkest, they're still divine. There is nowhere that God is not—that love, grace, and perfection are not. It's not really darkness. It's the absence of light. And there's hope and joy on the other side of all the things the soul signed up for. We grow when we learn about the not light, the not love, and the not grace. This duality is an illusion. All is well and always will be because God is on duty.

Q. Anything else?

A. I would like to thank you in gratitude. What a surprise! I have never been interviewed before. I am honored and blessed to have the invitation, to have the opportunity to show up without advanced notice and have it turn out beautifully. It was scary at first and yet beautiful in that duality. I can deal with both scariness and beauty because they are just frequencies passing through.

"The religious quest is ongoing. One where we never reach a final answer."
Dr. Lewis Ryder, Honorary Senior Lecturer in Physics, University of Kent

Dr. Lewis Ryder graduated in physics from Oxford University and obtained his Ph.D. in mathematical physics from Edinburgh University. After a SERC Fellowship at Durham and Oxford Universities, he went to the University of Kent at Canterbury in 1967 where he is an Honorary Senior Lecturer. He is the author of three books: *Elementary Particles and Symmetries*, *Quantum Field Theory*, and *Introduction to General Relativity*. His research interests are in geometrical aspects of particle theory and its parallels with general relativity. More recently, he is interested in the application of general relativity in the atomic— quantum— domain.

Q. What experiences put you on your spiritual path?
A. I wouldn't say any particular experience. I have always had a religious sense, a sense that there are important questions about how we should understand and live our lives. The different religions try to answer these questions in different ways.

Q. How did this sense change you?
A. It helped me develop a consistent view of the world. I think the religious quest is an ongoing one, one where we never reach a final answer. If we look at things properly, we get closer and closer to the notion of truth. But I am hesitant to use the word "truth" in a religious context because I'm suspicious of doctrinal expressions of truth. One difference between religion and disciplines like science, philosophy, and literature is that religious truths are not expressed in words.

They are not expressed in formulae or doctrine. They are just ways of being alive. Rather than rely on formulae and doctrines, we have to experience life in a direct way. It's in the way that Zen Buddhists talk. It's a direct perception of life itself, which is not translatable into words.

Q. What changes are you noticing about your life and the world?
A. Over a long period of time, I do see things differently. It's not a sudden revelation. Children have no problems understanding the world. They experience it directly. As they get older, they begin to ask questions about the world. They want to understand it in their own terms. Then it becomes very complicated. But with a bit of luck, as they get older they again return to the simplicity of directly understanding the world. As Christ said, "Become as little children." He didn't mean become childish. He meant returning to a direct encounter of the world.

Q. What changes are others noticing about you?
A. I wouldn't say they have noticed changes. They know that I am generally interested in these things and that I read a bit about them. It's not an obsession, but it is a serious interest. They would say that it's just part of my personality. I wouldn't say that over the years I have changed greatly. I'm pretty sure I'm similar now to a decade ago.

Q. What has been the most challenging part of your path?
A. I have always been aware—as most people have who take an intelligent interest in these things—that there seems to be a clash between science and religion. On an intellectual level, that is something that has always exercised me a bit—to try and understand what the nature of this clash is. That's more of an intellectual, rather than a personal, challenge. On a personal level, I don't think I have had immense difficulties, at least not ones I can put my finger on at the present. I am a fairly ordinary person. On the whole, things have gone all right. Some things haven't gone so well, some things have

gone better. I muck through as best I can. There's nothing really spectacular to report.

Q. What is your earliest memory? Why do you remember it?
A. When I was somewhere between eight and twelve years old, I remember my aunt saying, "Never think that people are talking badly of you." I have never forgotten that. It was such an interesting thing to say. It had never occurred to me before in those words. It also has a religious dimension to it—being ourselves, not paying too much attention to what others think, and not concluding that they think ill of us.

Q. Who are your mentors? What have you learned from them?
A. We are approaching something I see as characterizing the difference between the English and American outlooks on life. Americans think explicitly and directly in terms of personal experience—what the greatest influences on their lives have been. The English see things in slightly less personal terms. They don't ask themselves so much, "What am I doing? How am I living my life? How do other people see me? Am I achieving my goals?" They don't live in that way. What they do more of than Americans is sit back and watch the world go by and hope that they can find a place in it. I'm sure that English society is changing and it's changing in the American direction, but I don't belong to that generation. I see things in a more European context. I don't see things so readily in terms of personal encounters. Perhaps you might think I'm passing the buck, but I don't think I am doing that. I'm trying to answer your question as best I can but I'm not sure that's a satisfactory answer.

Q. Follow-up question: Is God a mentor in some way?
A. I was brought up in a Church of England household. I went to church every Sunday and I was musical, so I finished up playing the organ at that church and had to go every Sunday. That formed an important dimension in my life. The Church of England is like the Episcopal Church in America, where

the emphasis is partly on scripture, but only partly. There is some appreciation of spiritual values, which nonconformist traditions such as the Methodists and Baptists would not take as seriously. I grew up in a general Christian environment and that did have a big influence on me. It formed my outlook over a large number of years.

Q. What is the greatest challenge facing society?

A. The survival of the human race in a decent form over the next century is a really pressing question. The issues facing us are really great. One of them is global warming, which is a very serious problem. Unless something is done about it, it could result in a lot of conflict with poor countries being hit harder than rich ones. When people are deprived of things they need like food and water, they will fight over it so wars result. On top of that, there is the whole business of terrorism and the wrong sort of people getting hold of weapons. I think there is a very serious period coming up. Global warming may have the effect of unbalancing people and disturbing the peace and terrorists of creating havoc over the world in their different ways.

Q. Follow-up question: How can we best deal with what's coming?

A. What a leading question. Your President Obama is an absolutely excellent man. With him as President of the United States, I feel quite a bit happier than I have for some time. He cannot do it single-handedly, as he keeps saying. A lot of people need to understand these problems and go about trying to solve them in a rational and humane way.

Q. What advice would you give someone just starting his or her spiritual path?

A. I would start by breaking down the question and asking if there is a particular problem or thing they want to think about. If you just mention religious question or spiritual path, it is far too general. People might have very particular things they want to sort out in their minds or lives. Then we can try to isolate what that thing is and talk about it. The approach is more microscopic than global.

Q. What are your practices for connecting to your higher purpose?

A. I do not do any on a regular, systematic basis. I think that one of the problems is the word "God." What do we mean by God? That is a real problem. In the Christian tradition, God is not only the creator of the world, but also takes an individual interest in every human being. Now as far as the creation of the world is concerned, physics gives quite a convincing account of that and the hypothesis of God is nowhere needed. So to understand the creation of the world, we don't need the idea of God.

In a religious context, God is most powerful as a concept in talking about individual destiny, in talking about ourselves as individuals and how we live our lives and understand our situation. But the notion that there is a being outside the universe is one that scientists find extremely difficult to cope with—almost a contradiction in terms. I certainly find it difficult to cope with. If you look at the world and the things that happen, it is very implausible to say there is a God looking after us when there are earthquakes, tsunamis, and natural disasters that kill thousands of people. What's God doing at times like this? This notion of God is a very faulty one and it has to be supplanted by some other idea of God, which German theologians started talking about in the nineteenth century—the notion of God as being the ground of our being. When we talk about God, we are really talking about an essential part of our existence as individual people. That is a much more satisfactory way of talking about God. But then, of course, when you use that language, you are shedding the whole metaphysical and supernatural connotations that Christianity traditionally has employed.

Q. Follow-up question: Do you mean the historical Christ?
A. The whole quest for the historical Christ dates from that same time. It's all part of the same general investigations about what we mean by God and who Jesus is.

Q. How do you use these practices when you get out of balance?
A. I don't get cross very often. As I grow older, I get cross even less. When people say things that annoy me, I try to remain calm and do not respond. I have a rule that I shouldn't say anything until I have completely gotten over my anger. We should never say things to people when we are still agitated about them. We should wait until we are completely calm and have come to terms with the situation. Being angry doesn't happen all that often but when it does, that is my rule of thumb.

Q. How do you balance planning with remaining open to opportunity?
A. I think not to work too hard. When people work too hard, they become obsessed and engrossed in their work and that's a bad thing. We must always try to remain open to all the different experiences life has to offer, which is why I like keeping in contact with people like you. Life throws up excellent opportunities of getting to know different people and places. We must really try and always be open to these things. That means not getting engrossed in any one thing.

Q. If you received £100,000, how would you spend it?
A. This is a slightly off-track question. I really don't know. You're trying to find out what I would really want to spend some money on if I had some more. The trouble is that I'm not all that interested in money. I have most things that I want. I suppose my son doesn't have enough money. He lives in a very small house in Bristol. So I would like to give him enough money to buy a bigger house. Then my wife and I could also have a nice holiday or something like that.

Q. If you had thirty seconds with someone in an elevator, what three things would you tell the person to do to be joyful, peaceful, and whole?

A. It is a very personal question so it has to be a very personal answer. If I just met somebody in an elevator, I wouldn't know them. Any answer I gave wouldn't be addressing them as individuals. So I would ask the person why they are asking the question. What do they want most out of life? What do they feel they are lacking? As you said earlier, this is a very American question. Americans are really interesting. On the one hand, what I like about Americans is that you are optimistic, outgoing, and open—more open than Europeans. On the other hand, you worry more about things. You are never really content. Perhaps you see the converse, that Europeans are not very interesting because they are too unquestioning, too content with things. I would want to ask the person, "What's bugging you?" because I don't go around thinking in what ways my life could be better. It doesn't really worry me. I just get on with things.

Q. What books or resources have helped you the most? Why?

A. People have very different taste in books. Perhaps you and I have a bit of overlap in the sort of books that might appeal to us. But if you take people at random, then I'm not sure I could recommend a book because I am not sure they would like it at all. I'm reading a book about Sigmund Freud at present, which I find absolutely engrossing, but I couldn't recommend that to any old person because the number of people who are interested in that sort of thing is really rather small. I can't think of any book that I would recommend to absolutely everyone. I'd have to know what things appealed to people and what their interests were.

Q. Follow-up question: Would the Bible be something you would recommend?

A. You're quite right to cite the Bible. There is a book that has had a fantastic amount of influence over the world in the last 2,000 years. That is a book that one could say to people, "Why don't you try reading that and see how you get on?" The reason I did not say that is because it seems to me a bit like proselytizing. I come from a Christian tradition and if someone wants a book to help them and I say the Bible, then it seems as if I am recommending they take the same path I have. This may not be right for them. On the other hand, it might actually help them a lot.

People should be aware of many resources and they should do as much as they can to make their lives as varied as possible. I get a lot of happiness from going and seeing different places. Last weekend, I was in Scotland climbing mountains and had an absolutely wonderful time. It rained a lot, as it does in Scotland, but when it didn't rain, it was superb. I know a lot of people like nature and music. Life is full of all these helpful, pleasing things. The more people can discover different activities, the richer their lives will be.

Q. What would you like to be written on your tombstone?
A. I don't particularly want to be remembered because the people I know very well will remember me in the way they want. The people I know less well, like you, will have memories of me and I won't forget you either. And that's enough for me. A specific question about a tombstone . . . I just like simple ones with the name, dates of birth and death, and really no more.

Q. Anything else?
A. I think you are looking for something that is like a summary of how people should direct their thinking and being. I think the most important thing for all of us is to realize our full potential as individuals. That means not being selfish, not becoming attached to a logical formulation of religious ideas, and not becoming attached to one's own desires, but to respond individually and spontaneously to everything around us, including our enemies.

"It is through our desires and our humanity that we find God."
Elias Salem, A New Monday Life Coaching

Elias is happily married with five children. In the past, Elias has worked in the construction, retail, food and IT industries. Currently, Elias is an information technology freelancer and is also building his coaching practice, A New Monday. He is working towards helping other people discover their true calling and passion in life.

Q. What experiences put you on your spiritual path?
A. I grew up feeling depressed, with an absent father and dependent mother. I felt empty as I fed my mother's needs and sacrificed my own. Depression led me to search for theological and philosophical answers that would give life meaning. When I joined the Catholic lay movement, Communion and Liberation, I found the answers I was seeking. Father Luigi Giussani, the movement's founder, encouraged me to follow my heart. Now I know that it is through our desires and humanity that we find God, not in spite of them.

Q. How did these experiences change you?
A. Before, I felt like I was living in a shack, chained by depression and policed by God, who was just waiting for me to do something wrong. I believed the only way to avoid punishment was to forgo my needs and follow God's will. After being part of Communion and Liberation, I now am free to follow my heart's desires because they will lead me to God.

Q. What has been the most challenging part of your path?
A. The most challenging part has been other people's resistance to my way of life. As I stop worrying about what others

think, I become free. Also, my own resistance gets in the way sometimes because it seems too good to be true that I can follow my desires to God. Then I remember that there is a clear distinction between self-gratifying ego wants and service oriented heart desires. I know that the path of the heart is the path to God.

Q. What changes are you noticing about your life and the world?
A. I am happier and more carefree. I have a sense of meaning in my life. We all are here because we have a special part to play. My role is to reassure people that desire is okay because it opens our hearts to God. This encouragement puts smiles on their faces and helps me form deeper friendships. I see everyone as my companion.

Q. What changes are others noticing about you?
A. I smile more and am fun to be around. People want to spend time with me. I notice people asking me questions and seeking my advice.

Q. What is your earliest memory? Why do you remember it?
A. At age three, we moved into a new home. I remember being excited as I carried the legs of the dining room table into the house. Being depressed, I thrived on change and new things because they brought me pleasure.

Q. Who are your mentors? What have you learned from them?
A. Dan Miller, author of *48 Days to the Work You Love*. His coaching set me on the path of following my calling. I didn't actually start making changes until I joined my Communion and Liberation School of Community (www.clonline.org). Being a part of the community gives me the support I need to do what I love. Earl Nightingale's books, *The Strangest Secret* and *Lead the Field*, also help me shift into more positive thinking.

Q. What is the biggest challenge facing society?

A. Boredom. We are adventurous by nature and want to be challenged. By taking our hearts out of the picture, we have sought to satisfy this drive with money, materialism, sex, and drugs—none of which will sate us. We have become an increasingly detached society, with kids worshipping Nintendo and adults playing video games all night. When we return to our hearts and embrace our desires, life truly becomes adventurous.

Q. What advice would you give someone just starting his or her spiritual path?
A. First, that it's okay to be human and to desire. Take time to look at your desires and break them down so you can find their essence. Second, connect with people already on a spiritual path and ask them questions about how they got where they are. Third, find a community of witnesses who are on your spiritual path and who can support you. Faith is knowledge based on someone you trust witnessing the truth to you.

Q. What are your practices for connecting to your higher purpose?
A. My practices are participating in the Communion and Liberation group, writing in my journal, and being in silence. The group supports me in becoming the person I am meant to be, journaling helps me clarify my experiences, and silence allows me to rest in God.

Q. How do you use these practices when you get out of balance?
A. When I get out of balance, I step back, take a deep breath, and gain perspective. This approach helps me see that I don't always have control, so it's easier for me to accept things as they come without becoming upset or angry.

Q. How do you balance planning with remaining open to opportunity?

A. Every morning, I pray saying, "God, bring into my life the people I'm meant to meet, the situations I'm meant to be in, and the opportunities I'm meant to receive." When we open our hearts, God does everything in his power to make good things happen. We're in a bigger story with forces at work that guide us in our parts to play, like the characters in *The Lord of the Rings*.

Q. If you received $100,000, how would you spend it?
A. I would invest it in building my life coaching practice so I can be of greater service and live out my passion without needing to do other ventures to make ends meet.

Q. If you had thirty seconds with someone in an elevator, what three things would you tell the person to do to be joyful, peaceful, and whole?
A. Open your heart, accept your desires, and embrace reality and yourself as they are right now. Being fully present and living here and now brings great joy and peace.

Q. What books or resources have helped you the most? Why?
A. I find these John Eldredge books helpful because they talk about the heart and desire: *Wild at Heart: Discovering the Secret of a Man's Soul, Waking the Dead: The Glory of a Heart Fully Alive, The Journey of Desire: Searching for the Life We've Only Dreamed Of,* and *Desire: The Journey We Must Take to Find the Life God Offers.*

I like J.R.R. Tolkien's *The Lord of the Rings* and C. S. Lewis' *The Chronicles of Narnia* because they are good stories and people want to live inside of stories. Stories help us see the big picture and follow our passion. I also like Jack Canfield's *The Power of Focus: What the World's Greatest Achievers Know about the Secret of Financial Freedom and Success* because it offers practical advice and goes deeper than most success books.

Since truth is harmonic, music is a great resource. I listen to classical, chant, and even emo punk because it cries out for meaning, releases emotion, and reminds me where I came from.

Q. What would you like to be written on your tombstone?
A. "Elias was a truth seeker who moved us and made us think."

Q. Anything else?
A. Be open to life. If life didn't exist, what else would matter?

"Love Wins"

-Robbie Seay Band

"Sit in God's lap and allow yourself to be truly loved by him"
Linda Sloan, Author and Cofounder of The Transformation Group

Linda graduated from the University of Colorado, Boulder, with a Bachelor of Arts degree in psychology. She went to work as an account executive for a large insurance company and later was promoted to the home office as a recruiter and trainer for field sales and service representatives. Later, Linda joined her husband, Eric, as an employee benefits consultant specializing in customized, self-funded insurance plans. She also worked alongside him in restoration ministry, becoming an ordained marketplace pastor in 200Q. Together they founded The Transformation Group, a company whose purpose is to equip organizations to succeed in the fullness of God's plan. Linda has written her first book, *Reinventing the Wheel*, on transforming the marketplace through shifting business structure out of the traditional pyramid shape (control) into the shape of a wheel (collaboration). She has done extensive teaching on the subject.

Q. What experiences put you on your spiritual path?
A. I desperately needed God and he showed up where I needed him most. He restored and redeemed everything in my life that was falling apart. Difficult as those times were, I thank the Lord for them because I was able to see his power. Now that I have searched for the truth and learned to overcome, rather than be a victim, I can help others walk this path.

Q. How did these experiences change you?
A. God brought strength to my weak areas, helping me trust and feel secure in his power rather than my own. He healed, equipped, and prepared me to fulfill what he has called me to do.

Q. What changes are you noticing about your life and the world?
A. My faith has grown exponentially by knowing who God is and what he can do. The more I know of him, the more I am blown away by his vastness and immenseness. How much more of him there is! It's been a journey of stepping further and further into this place of faith.

Q. What changes are others noticing about you?
A. Knowing who I am in Christ transformed me from a victim to an overcomer. I stand in the authority of Christ and expect God to do miracles daily. For example, I often have the opportunity to pray for people and God delivers divine healing. I have watched God bring many individuals deliverance from blockages in their lives, deep emotional healing, as well as physical healing. One time, I prayed for someone and felt it was important to pray for God to heal her heart. As we completed the prayer, the individual shared that she was supposed to have open-heart surgery the next day. Two weeks later, she approached me at church to celebrate the doctor's report. She said that the doctor had done another test prior to beginning the surgery. To everyone's surprise, her heart was completely healed. The doctor couldn't understand it but said she did not need surgery. Glory to God!

Q. What has been the most challenging part of your path?
A. Really trusting God when I looked around and everything seemed to be totally falling apart. Sometimes God uses a situation that really takes us to the end of ourselves to bring us closer to him. I had to overcome the fear involved and finally be obedient to God no matter what. I'll never forget the time that I experienced the loving healing of God in my own life and my mother noticed a significant change in me. She saw such a huge change that she thought I had taken some type of antidepressant or something. I was able to share my testimony of God's incredible healing without any drugs or medication.

Q. What is your earliest memory? Why do you remember it?
A. At age three, my grandmother came to visit us for the summer. She always brought such wonderful gifts. I very innocently asked, "Grandma, did you bring us just a little something?" That year, she brought me a gorgeous yellow nightgown with layers of lacy petticoats. Now this nightgown was much too beautiful to simply sleep in, so I chose it as my gown to dance in as I listened to the Lennon Sisters on the Lawrence Welk Show. I danced for the entire neighborhood in front of our huge picture windows until my mother made me cover up and maintain some modesty. I think I remember it because of the joy I felt—joy for my grandparents visiting, joy for the lovely gift, and joy for the freedom to dance. Maybe this was a little like when King David danced in his underwear, filled with the joy of the Lord!

Q. Who are your mentors? What have you learned from them?
A. My mother taught me how to care for and really love people. My father taught me the importance of integrity as well as a strong work ethic and a spirit of excellence. Two incredible women of God taught me about my relationship in my walk with the Lord and in my understanding of how to flow in the prophetic gifting of hearing God's voice. They also taught me about spiritual warfare as addressed in Ephesians 6:12-13, "For we do not war against flesh and blood, but against principalities, against powers, against the rulers of the darkness of this age, against spiritual hosts of wickedness in the heavenly places. Therefore, take up the full armor of God that you may be able to withstand in the evil day, and having done all, to stand."

Q. What is the greatest challenge facing society?
A. The greatest challenge is our lack of spiritual understanding and relationship with the triune God. On a personal level, we see this manifest in many ways such as death, divorce, pain, and fear. On a global scale, we witness this in many ways, such as destruction, genocide, poverty, and war. As scrip-

ture says, "My people perish for lack of knowledge." (Hosea 4:6, Isaiah 5:13) I believe we are in a world that is perishing. When governments make decisions that contradict God's word, they set up their nations for destruction.

Q. What advice would you give someone just starting his or her spiritual path?
A. Start by sitting in God's lap and allowing yourself to be truly loved by him. Ask the Lord to show you what his plan is for your life and take time to prepare yourself for the fullness of it. Deliverance and healing are for everyone. God will lead you in the right time.

Q. What are your practices for connecting to your higher purpose?
A. God is so much a part of my life that I don't really think through the processes anymore. I am in ongoing conversation with him through prayer. I pray every morning and throughout the day, asking the Holy Spirit to direct my prayers. I also spend a lot of time reading scripture. Usually God will give me direct revelation through the Bible, especially with regards to my clients. When a person needs breakthrough, I'll ask God to show me what's going on and how I can best pray. My husband and I also take our relationship challenges to God in prayer. My relationship with the Lord is so beautiful that it gives me hope in every situation. I also like listening to worship music to feel God's presence.

Q. How do you use these practices when you get out of balance?
A. I repent, seek forgiveness, where appropriate, and pray for direction to move forward. Relationships are so important to me that I allow God into the places where I've messed up. My experience has been that he moves things beyond where they could have been had the issue not happened. This creates a better outcome.

Q. How do you balance planning with remaining open to opportunity?

A. I used to be very set in my schedule. I decided this was not necessarily a godly place for me to be. The Holy Spirit sometimes puts us out of order so we don't miss all that God wants to do in our lives. Now I use some structure because I am more productive that way, but I look forward to watching the Holy Spirit move in the midst of the structure. Flexibility allows for freedom, joy, and all of the things that are beyond what we can accomplish with our own power.

Q. If you received $100,000, how would you spend it?

A. I'd pray asking, "Lord, where do you want this blessing to go?" Then I'd wait for his answer. It's very likely that my husband and I would take our two children on a special vacation to simply rest, enjoy ourselves, and make memories. Then some of the money would most likely be given away. And some would be used to pay off debt. I address this topic of "coming out of Babylon" in my book. Many of us are tied to the Babylonian system and structure through debt. Financially freeing ourselves so we can have cash available is increasingly important as God lifts us out of our Babylonian structure and brings us into the time of Jubilee. I believe that all Christians must understand this critical time and the strategies that are emerging.

Q. If you had thirty seconds with someone in an elevator, what three things would you tell the person to do to be joyful, peaceful, and whole?

A. First, I would encourage them to accept Jesus Christ as their Lord and Savior. Then I would pray for them to receive the fullness of the baptism of the Holy Spirit with fire and power. Finally, I would encourage them to ask the Lord what his redemptive purpose is for their lives and pray for strategy to fulfill all that he has called them to do.

Q. What books or resources have helped you the most? Why?
A. I would recommend the Bible. Any other resource would depend on what's going on in the person's life at the time. When I am meeting with someone, I get a sense of what he or she is dealing with and I'll say, "Check out this book. It may give you some revelation or understanding." Each person within the body of Christ has a different assignment and all of them are critical. So until I know the specifics, there is no one place I would send someone except the Word.

Q. What would you like to be written on your tombstone?
A. I would like this passage from Isaiah 61:1-2, "The spirit of the Lord God is upon me, because the Lord has anointed me to preach good tidings to the poor; he has sent me to heal the brokenhearted, to proclaim liberty to the captives, and the opening of the prison to those who are bound; to proclaim the acceptable year of the Lord . . ." This is my assignment. So my prayer is to fulfill it without missing anything.

Q. Anything else?
A. I want to see the fullness of the God of the Bible operating outside of church buildings, in our daily lives and in everything we do, especially in the marketplace. This is where Jesus and his disciples spent most of their time and many people need to see miracles to believe. My husband and I are called to equip businesses and organizations so the Lord can fully dwell there. My book, *Reinventing the Wheel: God's Transfiguration of the Marketplace*, is for that part of the population that wants to bring transformation into their businesses and is willing to do whatever it takes to fulfill God's calling in their lives.

"Avoid spiritual shopping. Stick with one method and go deep."
Janet Solyntjes, The Center for Courageous Living

Janet Solyntjes, MA, has taught meditation and body awareness practices for over twenty years. She leads meditation and yoga retreats in the United States and Canada, is a Mindfulness-Based Stress Reduction teacher, a senior Shambhala Training director, and Adjunct Professor at Naropa University. She co-founded The Center for Courageous Living with her husband, Jeff Price. The center promotes the inherent goodness of individuals and groups by uncovering their basic health and well-being. These qualities are revealed through a mindful exploration of our many relationships in the world: to self, family, and community. Through this process, natural wisdom arises that guides the individual to be of service to others. Thus, the center's vision is to cultivate a healthy, sane, and caring society.

Q. What experiences put you on your spiritual path?
A. There were many small dots that eventually formed a line. In high school I was curious about various faiths, so my friends and I visited a different church every Sunday. Each had a unique texture. When I went to college, I took a Zen Buddhism class in which we did a brush painting. As I painted, I felt my body, mind, and energy shift, but quickly forgot the experience. In the winter of 1977, my friends had a Naropa Institute catalog and said they were going to attend the following summer. I said I would come too. Being around the school's founder, Chögyam Trungpa Rinpoche, and other Tibetan Buddhists was provocative. It shook me out of the status quo and led me to meditation, which served as a gateway to what would become a lifelong journey. At first I followed a secular meditation path because I was not interested in be-

ing Buddhist. I saw meditation and religious tradition as far apart. Years later, I began asking questions about Buddhism and exploring it as a path. Now I see the two as very similar.

Q. How did these experiences change you?
A. I became more of who I am as I peeled away layers of confused self, patterns that originally had wisdom but now existed only out of habit. It was like finally having the right amount of sunshine and water to grow. It's hard to differentiate how much of this uncovering would have happened as part of natural maturation. My guess is having a spiritual path made the experience richer and deeper. Now I'm much more comfortable with myself and kinder to others because I have identified and worked through some of my fears and self-judgments, which kept me separate and in pain. As my heart opened, I became more compassionate and was able to see the bigger picture beyond me. My interest in being open to all kinds of people evolved into a sense of being part of the whole human race. For example, when I hear about people suffering in other continents, it affects me. I'm not numb to it.

Q. What changes are you noticing about your life and the world?
A. Buddhist teachings on emptiness and illusion have allowed me to go back and forth between thinking I know the world and recognizing I haven't a clue. For example, I have lived in Boulder since 1978, yet still sometimes walk down the street and ask, "What is Boulder?" This inquisitiveness, along with meditation and bodywork, have helped me work with my inner energies. Relaxing my mind and releasing the holding in my body has opened gaps between my thoughts. I started seeing these gaps all over the place and realized I could free myself from habitual behavior and go in any direction. Students who come for stress reduction are not necessarily interested in finding the meaning of life. But they are curious about why it's hard to relax and why they have pain. The more I meditate (go within) and travel (go without), the more

I relate to different kinds of people without needing to know their cultural backgrounds, medical conditions, and so on. People all over the world are asking the same questions. We want to stop war but we won't if we keep going into some sense of difference—I'm American, you're Muslim.

Q. What changes are others noticing about you?
A. My mother and I are opening on our paths at the same time so we have more appreciation for each other and are able to vocalize it. Other than that, it's rare for friends and family to make comments. That's more of a teacher role. A few years ago, one of my teachers said, "I'm so proud of you. A lot of people would have given up, but you stayed." I think this was an acknowledgement of my whole path without having to call out specifics. When you stay in a spiritual community for a long time, you see people moving from student to teacher, and they see you. Not really a lot has to be said.

Q. What has been the most challenging part of your path?
A. The path is so exposing. In order to grow, I had to see where I was immature. This recognition is humbling and can lead, especially early on, to harsh self-criticism. For example, when I saw a childish pattern, I would judge myself saying, "I can't believe you are so fearful." Then I would want it to go away immediately. So I had to cultivate patience and believe that I could be something other than a scared little girl. The irony is that I was a professional dancer who could perform in front of thousands of people. Yet inside, I did not feel safe, especially in relationships.

Q. What is your earliest memory? Why do you remember it?
A. I remember being asked a similar question before, but my response is only an idea now. In the moment, I'm checking to see what my body feels. I have a vague memory of taking a dance class in kindergarten and giving a performance. I was sitting on stage doing something with my hands and feeling happy. Dance brings out such joy. I really love expres-

sion through movement, especially when accompanied by music. I smile just thinking about it.

Q. Who are your mentors? What have you learned from them?
A. • Chögyam Trungpa Rinpoche has had the greatest impact on my life through his teachings, community, and Naropa, the university he founded where I have taught (on and off) for twenty-five years. Other mentors include:

• Leslie Petteys, my college piano teacher, who encouraged me to stretch myself without ever pushing. For example, I performed a solo piano concert, something I never thought I would do. Her blurring the boundaries between mentor and friend supported me during a time I really needed it.

• Guy Duckworth, my graduate school professor, who taught me about communication, teaching, and being a member of a small group. In his group environments course I also learned how to be around a powerful, charismatic leader and still maintain my own individuality.

I feel grateful to many mentors, but these three stand out. Their ability to teach through indirect means helped me integrate ideas that were a big leap and led to my developing a larger view.

Q. What is the greatest challenge facing society?
A. We are experiencing a greater sense of global community and, simultaneously, a heightened sense of us versus them. For example, when I heard the Air France jet crashed, my eyes welled up, my heart opened, and I felt connected to everyone on the plane. In contrast, when some people heard the swine flu started in Mexico, they blamed the Mexicans as if it was their flu. When I moved into my house, the previous owner said wryly, "Garage door openers are the worst thing to happen to America. Now people drive in and close the doors without saying hi to their neighbors." So we have

this ironic isolation amidst great interconnectedness. We can use meditation and other practices to help us drop our guard and become one with each other. Being connected means more than logging onto the Internet.

Q. What advice would you give someone just starting his or her spiritual path?

A. Listen to the advice of the teacher to whom you are drawn, as well as that of other teachers in the lineage. Do the practices and know that you will not want to do them at times, especially when their newness fades. Avoid spiritual shopping. Stick with one method and go deep. If you stick with something for a while, you may find it's not right for you. In that case, change. But be discerning. Know that the fickle mind is going to come out in some way. It may come through as spiritual shopping or just the opposite, believing that everything your teacher says is true. Don't give away your spiritual path to someone else. Find it for yourself.

Q. What are your practices for connecting to your higher purpose?

A. I do formal practices in the Tibetan Buddhist, as well as the Shambhala tradition. They include meditation, visualization, yoga, and practices for rousing life force energy. Throughout the day, I exercise ongoing mindfulness. For example, this morning I did a White Tara practice at the bus stop where I imagined the people driving by in their cars as happy, healthy, and peaceful. I do this exercise to expand my mind and escape the dull dreaming state that can happen at a bus stop.

Q. How do you use these practices when you get out of balance?

A. I try not to push these states away so I can fully become them. The way to happiness is accepting things as they are without judging them. For example, when I am stressed, I stop, feel, and observe the thoughts running through my mind without getting attached to them. Then the moment becomes wisdom. If I'm out of balance for a while, it's usually because I have forgotten to stop, feel, and notice my thoughts. As a result, they keep feeding on themselves. You don't have to be a spiritual practitioner to suddenly realize your mind is racing. Sometimes I think, *I just need to go on retreat*. But that's a cop-out. It's like saying, "If only the outer world were different, I could settle my mind." If I can't deal with my mind in this situation, then the benefits of retreat won't last for long.

Q. How do you balance planning with remaining open to opportunity?

A. My native style is to plan but, as a dancer, I also improvise a lot. So I like to combine the two. For example, when I prepare to lead a retreat, I study and schedule out each day. But during the retreat, I prefer spontaneity. What I end up doing looks half like the plan and half in response to the students, environment, and my own inner calling. I'm at home with this style and extend it to my life, where I use a general framework but don't nail anything down unless I have to.

Q. If you received $100,000, how would you spend it?

A. First I would be shocked. Then I would give half to my favorite retreat center, the Shambhala Mountain Center, because so much of my growth as a teacher and spiritual practitioner has happened there. I would keep the other half because I am not working right now.

Q. If you had thirty seconds with someone in an elevator, what three things would you tell the person to do to be joyful, peaceful, and whole?

A. Appreciate your moments, whether they are happy or sad. They are the only moments you have and, in some way, are equal. Find a practice you love and let it bring you into your moments. I don't necessarily mean a spiritual practice, although that is what it is for me. Your practice could be anything—playing the guitar or going for a bicycle ride.

Q. What books or resources have helped you the most? Why?
A. I don't think I can generalize. I would take time to find out what motivates the person, the part of the journey that is most salient. Some easy book recommendations include:
• Pema Chödrön—Anything she has written because the way she talks about Buddhism and meditation is so accessible. My mom really likes her books.

• Jon Kabat Zinn—His writing is even more accessible because he takes mindfulness and puts it into everyday language. I would suggest different books by Jon depending on where the person is in the journey.

As far as resources, I would ask, "Do you do something to keep your mind and body in harmony?" Being able to wake up to the world and each other has to do with mind-body connection. People usually know what they need to establish this link. They sometimes just want to be reminded. However, when people tell me they need to meditate, half the time I don't believe them. Our culture is so motion oriented that we find it hard to sit still. When we do, it can be painful, or we grow restless or fall asleep after only a few minutes.

Q. How do you respond to someone who feels his or her path is the only right one?
A. We hear advice like, "Just remain in love," but we cannot maintain this state without practice. For example, if one person says to another, "You're going to hell," then that person is no longer in a state of love. This illustration shows how our true nature can get confused by what we are taught. When I hear world leaders use black-and-white terms, I feel the pain and confusion beneath the surface, almost like a firm grasping onto a limited notion of who they believe they are. I respond by holding a larger space for the pain and confusion because I realize it's not the person's fault. Usually many generations of conditioning are involved. Recently I jokingly asked my niece, a born again Christian, "So, do you think I am

going to hell?" She responded by giving a rehearsed answer that was not from her heart. If I could get her to say her true feelings—that I am going to hell—it might be a step forward.

Q. What do you think of the concept that my enemy is my lover?

A. When we have an experience of enemy, whether external or internal, it's an invitation to go deeper and join the lover part. Because we feel so strongly, we have the juicy energy needed to merge with it, unlike times when we feel indifferent. For example, I recently reacted to someone with whom I find it difficult to communicate. I could justify my feelings based on this person's behavior but that would deny this individual's basic goodness. As the Dalai Lama says, "Just like you, they want happiness. No different." So when we bring happiness—even to an enemy—we merge with the lover part. The aggression and fear that separates us is gone and we melt into the moment. In Thich Nhat Hanh's book, *Anger*, he offers, "If someone insults you, give a gift in your mind." This cuts the habitual way of reacting. Sometimes we think, *I'm so peaceful and loving*. Then boom, something happens to get us out of sorts. When things are peachy keen, we're probably not maturing. These booms give us a path to work with. As Hanh's example shows, he strengthened his compassion by making the enemy lover.

Q. What would you like to be written on your tombstone?

A. I will honor the Buddhist tradition and not have my body moved for three days so people can practice with my corpse in the room. I have a sense that the mind continues on after the body ends. I then will be cremated and have my remains brought up to a hillside at the Shambhala Mountain Center. I know that my life has been of benefit, so I don't need to make a statement. Buddhist training has taught me both the preciousness and fleeting nature of life, that I can do so much to help others in one lifetime but that I'm also not that important. Even with my own departed friends, I find myself forgetting their names. So let it *all* go—the sense of success and failure, fame and anonymity.

"I receive strength from God and pour it into others."
Terri Starck, LifePoint Strategies

Terri Starck is a strategist at heart. Terri asks the right questions to clarify your goals, knows what it takes to increase profitability, works with you to develop a path forward that builds on your leadership strengths, challenges and encourages you to live up to your potential. Terri has twenty years of experience including: starting and running her own successful business (twice), directing leaders, facilitating large and small groups, implementing strategic planning and calendaring, and doing computer programming and training. She has a record of accomplishment in coordinating and planning large strategic events. Her varied experience gives her the skill to tackle the diverse businesses she currently serves. Terri's strategies enable you to implement your professional vision and all while living Life with a Point.

Q. What experiences put you on your spiritual path?
A. I grew up Christian and, during my teens, tried to have it both ways—my way and God's way. In college, I joined the Inter-Varsity Christian Fellowship where I learned what it meant to lead a Christian life. Now I see the power of God moving through everyone, regardless of faith background. As a strategic coach, it is my privilege to receive strength from God and pour it into others.

Q. How did these experiences change you?
A. I continually become stronger and more grounded. I have the freedom to be me and you have the freedom to be you. God is working through us exactly as we are right now.

Q. What has been the most challenging part of your path?
A. I have gone through a reconciliation process with God. Early

in life, I received Christianity as rules—right and wrong ways of doing things. With a better understanding of grace, I now recognize that no one has all the answers. When we get to heaven, God will extend his grace and lovingly say, "You tried your best, but here's how it really is."

Q. What changes are you noticing about your life and the world?
A. When I pour God's strength and power into others, I feel humble and free. It's all about freeing people to be who they are meant to be and allowing myself to do the same.

Q. What changes are others noticing about you?
A. I'm more fun because I'm comfortable in my own skin. If you had interviewed me a year ago, I might have asked what other people said before giving my answer. I didn't want to be wrong. Now life is not an if-then-else statement. It's about being who I am and sharing my gifts.

Q. What is your earliest memory? Why do you remember it?
A. I don't remember much about my childhood because my family moved a lot. When we settled in a new place, I would scope it out and do the right things to fit in. This adaptation strategy led to fear around not being included. As an adult, I keep letting go of this fear so I can eventually pull out its root.

Q. Who are your mentors? What have you learned from them?
A. My husband Brian, who has stood by me and has full confidence in me. He shows such high ethics and values in how he lives his life every day. Anne and Kenny Moore, who taught me about God's grace. My mom, whose quiet contentment and strength always communicated her love, despite external circumstances. Jesus, who gave himself for us and showed us how to live.

Q. What is the biggest challenge facing society?
A. The media's over-dramatization of world events. It scares

people and they contract in fear, limiting their potential. When people contract, they cannot receive God's abundance. This hurts the world because they have less to give. My gift is pouring encouragement into others so they can live their lives more fully.

Q. What advice would you give someone just starting his or her spiritual path?
A. Read the Bible, especially the red letter edition in which Jesus' words are printed in red ink. I am studying the red letter because I want to know with whom Jesus spoke, what he said, and what he was telling me right before he died.

Q. What are your practices for connecting to your higher purpose?
A. In the morning, I pray by quieting myself before God and listening. Throughout the day, I am sensitive to what he wants me to say or do so I can best serve others. I also read the Bible and other books, and ask questions when talking with people.

Q. How do you use these practices when you get out of balance?
A. I stop, look into the other person's heart, and then respond. It's important to remain present and come from good intention. This is my perfect world practice; I often fall short.

Q. How do you balance planning with remaining open to opportunity?
A. I am a planner. Right now, I'm building room in my schedule to spend more time with my children, just having fun and relaxing. However, I am open to God changing my plan. For example, I met someone this weekend that I am excited to work with and it totally deviates from my plan. However, I know it's from God, so it's okay.

Q. If you received $100,000, how would you spend it?

A. I would give away ten percent, asking God where he wants it to go. I would use eighty percent to pay off debt and the remaining ten percent to take a great family vacation.

Q. If you had thirty seconds with someone in an elevator, what three things would you tell the person to do to be joyful, peaceful, and whole?
A. Know who you are, where you are going, and how you will get there. Also, observe what gets in your way and work to resolve it.

Q. What books or resources have helped you the most? Why?
A. Books: The Bible is the most important. Other books include *The Purpose Driven Life*, by Rick Warren, *The Shack*, by William P. Young, and *The Last Word on Power*, by Tracy Goss.

Resources: My personal relationship with God and my pastor, Steve Harling, who helps me connect with God every Sunday.

Q. What would you like to be written on your tombstone?
A. "She was born here, she died here, but her life was in the dot, dot, dot. Her life was lived pouring into others all the gifts God gave her." It's sad when people don't know their talents. Wouldn't it be great if our gifts were written above our hearts?

Q. Anything else?
A. Our relationship with God is dynamic. It is life itself. With God, we have freedom and abundance. My coaching clients experience amazing results because they come from God. I pour life into my clients, they pour life into others, and the benefits just multiply and multiply.

"God is my source of inspiration."
Eddie Yau, Secondary English Teacher, Pentecostal Lam Hon Kwong School

Eddie was born and raised in Hong Kong. He is married, has two children, and has been teaching in Hong Kong since 1983.

Q. What experiences put you on your spiritual path?
A. I learned about Jesus in grade school, but did not personally experience him until university when he showed me that my inferiority complex was preventing me from accepting others and their opinions. I could not accept them because I could not accept myself. When I felt God's unconditional love, I became comfortable with who I am and began taking part in activities, which gradually built my self-confidence.

Q. How did these experiences change you?
A. Before experiencing Christ, I was introverted and wouldn't let people get close to me. After being liberated, I gradually opened up and allowed more people into my life.

Q. What has been the most challenging part of your path?
A. To accept God's plan for my life without judging events as successes or failures. For example, I applied to be the Vice Principal of the school where I work and did not receive the promotion. At first, I was a bit disappointed, but now I realize it wasn't what God wanted for me.

Q. What changes are you noticing about your life and the world?
A. Hong Kong is a hectic place where people work around the clock. In the past, I focused only on my career and family. Now I make time to give and receive kindness by contacting friends and participating in my church men's group. My four

Christian brothers and I meet monthly to share our lives, exchange ideas, and pray for loved ones. This kind of sharing among men was unimaginable a few years ago, when we were confined to our work.

Q. What changes are others noticing about you?
A. A Christian brother I have known for ten years commented that I express myself with greater ease. I even disagree with him, something I shied away from before due to his articulate, outspoken nature. His remark means a lot because when we first served as student mentors together, I was introverted and didn't speak much.

Q. What is your earliest memory? Why do you remember it?
A. Childhood usually is one of the happiest times in life. Not so for me. My parents had a poor relationship and my mother sometimes threatened to commit suicide. I feared coming home because I wasn't sure she'd still be there. When I was nine, our relatives offered to take us to the department store. I so treasured this rare opportunity that I went in my undershirt rather than change into clothes and risk losing the chance. I was embarrassed when people pointed at me on the store's escalator, but I endured it so I could see the world.

Q. Who are your mentors? What have you learned from them?
A. God is the most important source of inspiration. He speaks to me during church and I write down what he says and do what he asks. I'm also inspired by Reverend Pao and another church member, Paul Man, both of whom have cancer. Despite their illnesses, they continued to do God's will—Rev. Pao by caring for youth, and Paul by living happily while preparing to return to our heavenly home. Also, when I was young, my uncle inspired me by saying, "Family is the most important." Now, as a father, I place family first.

Q. What is the biggest challenge facing society?

A. The biggest challenge is the disintegration of the family and the sensationalism of the media, which contributes to it. Without parental guidance, young people fall into drugs, sex, and violence to deal with unhappiness. Sometimes they harm others without regard to consequence—school shootings, gang fights, and son on. We need to restore our families and encourage the media to set a better example.

Q. What advice would you give someone just starting his or her spiritual path?
A. Reflect on your life, pray for guidance, and listen to your inner voice. As in Proverbs 9:10, "Knowing God is the beginning of true wisdom." Also, follow the Golden Rule, "Do unto others as you would have them do unto you."

Q. What are your practices for connecting to your higher purpose?
A. Prayer is the easiest way to connect with God. On my way to work, I look at the sky and pray about my concerns. On Sundays, God gives me guidance during the sermon or through Bible verses. I also connect with God through sharing with other Christians, like at our recent church men's retreat. The Holy Spirit liberated us to speak our minds and build strong relationships.

Q. How do you use these practices when you get out of balance?
A. I pray to God when I feel helpless or things don't work out. For example, when my children want something I don't approve of, they grow quarrelsome. At first, I am angry, but then put my faith in God and know everything will be all right. Similarly, I worked to get a remedial class put in our school because it is more effective than giving students extra lessons. Parents' concerns about labeling and limited resources stopped my efforts. Initially, I was disappointed, but then gave it to God and felt peace.

Q. How do you balance planning with remaining open to opportunity?
A. I wait for God's guidance rather than doing my own planning. For example, when people left Hong Kong before the sovereignty changed to China, I stayed because I didn't hear God calling me to leave. My openness to hearing God derives from my difficult childhood. I never had great ambitions, only to be happy and do my best. My wife Helen handles our long-term planning.

Q. If you received $100,000, how would you spend it?
A. I would put it in the bank and spend it when needs arise or invest it when opportunity comes.

Q. If you had thirty seconds with someone in an elevator, what three things would you tell the person to do to be joyful, peaceful, and whole?
A. I would say to each person, "Let's pray for guidance." Everyone's situation is unique, to be entrusted to God.

Q. What books or resources have helped you the most? Why?
A. Sermons and hymns are the greatest resources. For example, hymns such as "What a Friend We Have in Jesus" and "When I Survey the Wondrous Cross" move me to tears. I don't get as much from books because it's difficult to make time to read them unless they are part of my men's group or my couples' cell group. We finished, *The Purpose Driven Life*, by Rick Warren, two years ago. One particularly impactful passage said, "If you want to know why you were placed on this planet, you must begin with God. The world's wisdom is just speculation." Another good book is *The Message: The Bible in Contemporary Language*, by Eugene H. Peterson

Q. What would you like to be written on your tombstone?
A. "Eddie was a dutiful son, a caring father, a responsible teacher, and a true Christian who now rests in heaven."

Q. Anything else?

A. As it says in John 15:5-8, "I am the vine; you are the branches. If you remain in me and I in you, you will bear much fruit; apart from me you can do nothing. If you do not remain in me, you are like a branch that is thrown away and withers; such branches are picked up, thrown into the fire and burned. If you remain in me and my words remain in you, ask whatever you wish, and it will be done for you. This is to my Father's glory, that you bear much fruit, showing yourselves to be my disciples."

Also, though my mom is not yet Christian, I am grateful for her unconditional love and support, which helps me understand the love of our heavenly Father in concrete ways.

ACKNOWLEDGEMENTS

I would like to thank the following people who have made a difference in my life. To Celina Moore Barton, Stephany Buchicchio, Jennifer Stark, Geetanjali Chander, Signe Kurian, and Ruby Mayeda for being true friends and for teaching me about love. To Nancy Mercer, Barry Kopecky, Peter Rutland, Tony Daley, Robert J. Thomas, and Denise Darringrand for being outstanding teachers and mentors. To Dr. John Upledger, Dr. Charles Radbill, Dr. Jim Kerner, Jamy Faust, and Felice Lazarus for being exceptional healers and for helping me recover from my injury. To Rev. Diana Peters at Intercession Episcopal Church and Donna Visocky of BellaSpark Productions for being spiritual lights and for giving me the chance to write. To Gary Zukav, Linda Francis, and everyone in the Authentic Power Program for being in spiritual partnership with me and for helping me live courageously. To my CranioSacral Therapy clients for teaching me so much about beingness. To my grandmother Sophia, my husband Jasper, and my son Trevor for being so supportive and loving.

I also would like to thank all the spiritual leaders who generously gave their time to participate in this project. Their wisdom, courage, and willingness to share made this book possible. I especially am grateful to Brian Schwartz, Founder of 50 Interviews, for giving me the opportunity to author this book, Linda M. Potter, for writing such a humorous and insightful foreword, Melanie Mulhall for doing a marvelous editing job, and Dave Block for introducing me to Brian.

Finally, I would like to express my heartfelt gratitude to spiritual leaders, past and present, who inspire me every day: Jesus, Buddha, Lao Tzu, the Dalai Lama, Mother Teresa, Gandhi, Saint Teresa of Ávila, Saint John of the Cross, The Desert Fathers, Mungo Park, Joan of Arc, Stanford Addison, Christopher Reeve, Dick and Rick Hoyt, and the people of Nepal, Tibet, and China.

I send love and gratitude to all sentient beings. We are one. Thank you, Tuula Fai

ABOUT THE AUTHOR

Tuula Hoiska Fai is an author, speaker, seminar leader, and CranioSacral Therapist with fifteen years of experience in the human development field. She is the author of the highly acclaimed book, *Seek the Lover Within*. This book is the first in the 50 Interview series. Tuula gives presentations around the world on spirituality, personal growth, and healing to audiences including corporations, civic organizations, and individuals. Her passion is helping people achieve a state of oneness in which they follow their calling and devote their lives to service. Her own journey began when a debilitating all-over body injury encouraged her to heal herself holistically almost twenty years ago. You can contact her at tuula@ascendancehealing.com.

Prior to this work, Tuula was a marketing director and management consultant for Fortune 500 companies such as IBM, Oracle, and KPMG. She earned her MBA from Georgetown and her BA from Wesleyan University.

Stay up to date with Tuula and her latest interviews through her blog

spiritual.50interviews.com

Tuula Fai, MBA, CST, NCTMB
CranioSacral Therapist
303-909-4582
www.tuulafai.com
tuula@ascendancehealing.com

ABOUT 50 INTERVIEWS

50 Interviews is a publisher of books, CDs, videos, and software that serve to inform, educate, and inspire others on a wide range of topics. Timely insight, inspiration, collective wisdom, and best practices derived directly from those who have already succeeded. Authors surround themselves with those they admire, gain clarity of purpose, adopt critical beliefs, and build a network of peers to ensure success in that endeavor. Readers gain knowledge and perspective from those who have already achieved a result they desire.

Imagine a university where not only does each student get a textbook custom tailored to a curriculum they personally designed, but where each student literally becomes the author!

The mission of 50 Interviews is to provide aspiring, passionate, driven people a framework to achieve their dreams of becoming that which they aspire to be. Learning what it takes to be the best in your field; directly from those who have already succeeded. The ideal author is someone who desires to be a recognized expert in their field. You will be part of a community of authors who share your passion and who have learned firsthand how the *50 Interviews* concept works. A form of extreme education, the process promises to transform you into that which you aspire to become.

If you are interested in learning more, I would love to hear from you! You can contact me via email at: brian@50interviews.com, by phone: 970-215-1078 (Colorado), or through our website:

www.50interviews.com

All my best,
Brian Schwartz
Creator of *50 Interviews*

OTHER 50 INTERVIEWS TITLES

Additional topics based on the *50 Interviews* model that have already been released or are in development:

Athletes Over 50
by Don McGrath, Ph.D.

Young Entrepreneurs
by Nick Tart

Attraction Marketers
by Rob Christensen

Scientists
by David Giltner, Ph.D.

Physicians in Transition
by Rich Fernandez, MD

Property Managers
by Michael Levy

Professional Speakers
by Laura Lee Carter and Brian Schwartz

Successful Jobseekers
by Gordon Nuttall

Video Marketers
by Randy Berry

Spiritualists
by Tuula Fai

Financial Planners
by Allen Duck

Entrepreneurs
by Brian Schwartz

Success Franchisees
by Leslie Lautzenhiser

Tap into the collective wisdom at:
www.50interviews.com

www.ingramcontent.com/pod-product-compliance
Lightning Source LLC
Chambersburg PA
CBHW030311080526
44584CB00012B/525